SARAH STYLE

GALLERY
BOOKS

New York   London   Toronto   Sydney   New Delhi

G

Gallery Books
A Division of Simon & Schuster, Inc.
1230 Avenue of the Americas
New York, NY 10020

First Gallery Books hardcover edition November 2014

GALLERY BOOKS and colophon are registered trademarks of Simon & Schuster, Inc.

For information about special discounts for bulk purchases, please contact Simon & Schuster Special Sales at 1-866-506-1949 or business@simonandschuster.com.

The Simon & Schuster Speakers Bureau can bring authors to your live event. For more information or to book an event, contact the Simon & Schuster Speakers Bureau at 1-866-248-3049 or visit our website at www.simonspeakers.com.

Interior design by Rose Pereira
Jacket design by Rose Pereira
Room photos by Stacey Brandford
Portrait photos by Brandon Barré

Manufactured in the United States of America

10 9 8 7 6 5 4

Library of Congress Cataloging-in-Publication Data is available.

ISBN 978-1-4767-8437-3

DEDICATION

This book is dedicated to my family.

Thanks to all of you, home is my happy place
because it's where we are together.

To my parents, who taught me to appreciate art,
history, architecture, design, craftsmanship, style,
and creativity, and imbued my spirit with a passion
for beautiful objects and interiors.

You encouraged me to chart my own path
and build a career doing what I love.

To my husband, Alexander, who encourages, nurtures,
and fuels my creative spirit, champions my ideas with
blind faith, and inspires me to always go further.

You take me places where the skies are always blue,
no matter what the weather on the ground, and there
is no better adventure than life with you!

To my daughters, Robin and Fiona, who dazzle, delight,
and amaze me daily with their sweet, joyful creations
and unbridled enthusiasm and zest for life.

You have inspired me to design homes that are
youthful and happy, and you have filled
our home with joy and love.

XO
Sarah

CONTENTS

INTRODUCTION vii

INTRODUCTION

My goal is to create interiors for modern living that are informed by a classic perspective with timeless appeal. In order to design spaces that work for who we are today, I think it's important to reflect on where we've been and how we got here, to think about how we want to live today and into the future, and what we want to live with. This blend of past, present, and future, and the curation of materials, finishes, furniture, and art is what makes a house a home, and inevitably drives the design process and the path that any renovation or redecoration project takes.

I strive to make every home a genuine reflection of its inhabitants and provide a backdrop for the stories that will be told within it. No matter how simple or grand, your home is a sanctuary, and you have the power to define how you want to live in it. Over the course of five television series, I've tackled more than 300 rooms, and I've been given the opportunity to explore a wide variety of styles, palettes, and architectural influences according to each client's needs and tastes. My signature style is not always immediately recognizable by a colour or a theme (though I do certainly have my favourites . . .), but I feel there's a consistent style in how I approach design and the mix of elements I infuse in any space.

If I were to distill my design aesthetic down to the most simple recipe or formula, I would describe the ingredients and the ratio for their use as follows — my favourite rooms are . . .

One part masculine : one part feminine (since I often work with couples and believe in a democratic design process)
One part vintage or antique : one part new and now
One part traditional : one part contemporary
One part bold and exciting : one part calm and reserved
One part colourful : one part neutral
And, of course, one part practical : one part indulgent, exotic, whimsical, or fun.

Breaking hundreds of fully designed rooms down into a succinct list might be overly simplistic, but *Sarah Style* is my way of sharing what I've learned in my design career about the concepts that work and the ideas that endure. Design should be accessible and enjoyable. My goal is to deliver insights and advice, tips and inspiration to help you achieve the best results in your home, and to give you the confidence and enthusiasm to make your home everything you want it to be. Sarah Style is divided into chapters by type of room to allow you to peruse a variety of homes and see which styles and ideas speak to you. I hope you will find helpful suggestions and insider knowledge to make your planning process run smoothly, and make every project you tackle a triumphant expression of personal style — your personal style!

THE
ENTRY

I think of the entry, foyer, or front hall of your home as a sort of calling card for style. Open the door, cross the threshold, and the first room you encounter sets the tone for what to expect in the rest of the house. Whether your style is formal or casual, contemporary or traditional, the scene is set as soon as the door swings open. Yet these "front of house" areas are often overlooked and considered merely a transition zone to more important and grander areas. Forget the fact that you don't lounge, eat, entertain, or sleep in your entrance and embrace your ability to create a first impression that speaks volumes about the design direction of your home.

FASHIONABLE FRONT HALL

Period details and traditional accoutrements are often eliminated in the pursuit of contemporary city chic style, but this home proves that a renovation plan can embrace the old while ushering in the new to achieve a sympathetic blend that's well suited to modern family life.

GO WILD ↠

If you're holding on to a family heirloom and wondering how to breathe new life into an antique frame, try using a big, bold print. Victorian lady's and gentleman's chairs can seem dated and dour in fussy needlework coverings, but a large zebra print offers a contemporary juxtaposition of then and now, while presenting a striking sculptural silhouette in the entry.

MIX IT UP ↠

The appeal of buying an old house lies in its old-world charm and character. But respecting heritage doesn't mean you need to live in a historical time capsule. Maintain the traditional architecture of the house as a framework and then infuse contemporary spirit with decorating flourishes such as wallpaper, carpeting, lighting, and accessories.

HANDSOME TRANSIT HUB

In a house with a centre hall plan, the entry and adjoining hallway are continually in use as the conduit for all traffic through the house. In newer homes, these spaces can be rather large in scale and need to be considered as a proper room, with a distinct scheme and appropriate furnishings and art. With wide doorways leading to adjoining rooms, the entry hall is constantly in view, and its design should support the decor of the principal rooms. To add polish and panache to a suburban builder home, I relied on a neutrally grounded palette and furnished it with an impactful collection of pieces to represent the home's transitional style.

USE AN ANCHOR
Instead of a light and breezy console table that inevitably invites clutter and chaos, you can opt for a storage-savvy credenza or sideboard to keep clutter in the front hall to a bare minimum. Sleek wood doors and drawers can hide the trappings of daily life behind an exotic veneer, and a long tabletop surface allows room for elegant displays as well. With a bowl for keys, a tray for mail, and a few fresh blooms, the tone is set for order in the house.

POINTS OF LIGHT
Play up your opportunity to mix and match lighting for dramatic effect. Instead of a runway of basic pot lights, install a combination of pendants and sconces to illuminate with interest. Cut-glass lanterns cast a decorative pattern on the ceiling, while candle-arm sconces help break up large wall planes and bring illumination down to a lower level.

DARE TO BE DIFFERENT
There's no better place for an engaging piece of art than the entry, and placing a scene-stealing showpiece in the hall sets the stage for drama. The diagonal axis of this resin-coated photo has an imposing yet engaging and unexpected effect.

MIX, DON'T MATCH
If your look blends new and old elements with traditional and contemporary angles, lean on fabrics to reinforce your concept. A traditional crewel-embroidered linen with a vine motif gets an edgy and zingy update from a zigzag pillow rendered in similar hues.

DRAW THE LINE
To create a unified flow of flooring materials, you may want to use hardwood in your main entry area. Installing stone is also an option, but since the price to install marble is significantly higher than the price of wood, you'll likely be looking to pare back the size of the installed area. To ensure you've got a safe zone for wet footwear to land, I'd suggest installing a pad of stone across the width of your entry that extends about 4 or 5 feet into the hall. This way you can splurge on an interesting showpiece variety of stone to add drama and durability while making a good first impression.

UNDERSTATED ELEGANCE

Don't let your stair hall go unnoticed as a bland transition area between principal rooms and private spaces. Pay a little attention to this daily circulation zone and add a few little touches that will instill a sense of visual delight as you ascend and descend the stairs each and every day. A compact table here, a patterned wallpaper there, and a collection of intricately detailed prints will take your stair to another level.

OUTLINE YOUR PLAN ➟

When installing new hardwood floors, you've got an opportunity to create art underfoot. Instead of arranging strips of wood in straight lines, you can opt for a custom-laid marquetry pattern to introduce traditional elegance underfoot. Painstakingly installed one piece at a time, this old-world technique requires a skilled craftsman with plenty of patience. If your plan is to finish your floors with a natural clear coat instead of stain, you can accentuate the border of the room by installing a narrow strip of wood in a lighter colour from a different species.

DRESS IT UP ✐

Adding wallpaper to your stair hall brings pattern and texture to an area that might otherwise seem a tad lacklustre. Since wallpaper can be costly to purchase and install, you'll want to get the maximum life span out of it with minimum concerns about durability. By adding a chair rail profile about 32 inches above the height of the baseboards, you can achieve a two-tone wall treatment by painting the lower section, which is often prone to scrapes and bumps from traffic.

TRANQUIL VESTIBULE

Even a compact city home needs a good line of defense against clutter and chaos at the front door. With a few simple tricks, you can maintain order in the house and put your best foot forward when guests come calling.

HAVE A SEAT ⇥

The addition of an upholstered element lends a softer touch to an area outfitted with hard surfaces. A bench is a welcome addition to any foyer if you have the space — being able to perch while you pull boots on or off is handy. A light design with show wood legs will give you space to tuck boots underneath, or baskets for extra storage.

GO ALL THE WAY ↕

A full-length mirror isn't the first element you'd put on the list of things to buy for your entryway, but perhaps it should be since this mirror proves its value from both a decorative and functional purpose. (This one offers the added bonus of reflecting a sight line into the adjacent living room, making the hall feel more open and spacious.)

BE READY FOR ANYTHING ⇥

When you live in a climate that experiences all four seasons, you need to plan for the worst Mother Nature can deliver. Snow, salt, rain, and mud come with the territory, so it's wise to start with a foundation that can handle it all. I am a big proponent of a stone area in the front hall. If your front door is also your main entry point, it's a good idea to consider a honed stone material that won't become slippery when wet. Vein-cut limestone lends a contemporary look thanks to the horizontal striations in the stone, and the muted neutral palette ensures that it will always look presentable no matter what is tracked in.

HOLLYWOOD MODERN

A compact entryway can have all the zing and wow of a grander entry area. Don't be fooled into thinking your pint-sized space can't make a big impact statement, and channel your focus towards making the most of every surface to set the scene for style.

▬▬▬

LOOK DOWN ➻

Help a small entryway make a big style statement by focusing the attention on the floor with a dynamite geometric tile pattern in three shades of marble. Ask your tile supplier if they are able to custom-cut natural-stone tiles to the dimensions of your choice, as some suppliers can do this for a slight additional charge. The 12-by-12-inch tiles were chosen in three shades of light, medium, and dark to complement the tones in a large-scale painting on the hall wall. White marble was combined with charcoal and tan marble in a two-to-one ratio, and then the tiles were sliced diagonally from corner to corner to create triangular pieces. Achieving a dramatic tile pattern will take a bit of planning to perfect the layout and pattern, but it's definitely worth the effort.

CHECK THE FORECAST ➻

Heading out without your umbrella can lead to soggy results, so keeping it close to the door is a good idea. If you can't seem to find a stylish umbrella stand that appeals to your modern sensibility, consider using a readily available (and often inexpensive) large column vase as a clear and crisp catchall for your rainy-day collection.

WARM WELCOME

For those of us living in houses with a front door that opens onto the street, the options for finishes in an entry hall need to be practical and durable. If you live in an apartment or a condominium, the worry about wet outdoor shoes and wear and tear is alleviated, and the entry hall can be dressed in materials intended to set the scene and provide an inviting welcome at the front door.

ADD A FRENCH ACCENT ⬍
An antique French bombe chest with intricate ormolu mounts sets the tone for sophisticated elegance in the foyer. With a wide marble top and two deep drawers, a formal piece like this is both a beautiful and practical choice for your front hall. It offers plenty of surface area to set down keys or the mail, and some additional storage to keep necessities tucked away out of sight.

LIGHTEN UP ⬈
When indulging in fine furniture and gilded decorative objects, you may want to pull back the reins to keep your hall from going over-the-top in the decadence department. A delicately coloured cream and pale yellow, wide-striped wallpaper is a soothing foil to the intricacy and opulence of the chest and mirror, providing a linear backdrop to add a more casual note to the formal elements it frames.

GO AROUND ➻
A centre hall table makes a stately impression if you've got a large enough entry to accommodate it. Instead of regarding a piece of furniture in the middle of the room as a blockade to traffic flow, think of the circular profile as being similar to a roundabout on the road. Since there are no hard edges to bump into, people will just move around the table while it stands proudly in the room. Dress it with flowers and you'll feel happy to be home every time you open the door.

DEAL WITH YOUR HANG-UPS ➻
Not every home is designed with an ample front-hall closet, but that needn't discourage you from finding a workable solution to consume coats and hats at the front door. As an alternative to constructing a simple hall closet out of frame and drywall, consider how you could allocate the funds toward a functional focal point. This library cabinet has ample space inside, and forward-facing hanging rods ensure coats don't get dropped in a pile on the floor.

THE
LIVING
ROOM

My living room is my favourite room in the house. It's the one I associate with happy days, quiet nights, celebrations, and being together as a family. I believe in living rooms that are warm and inviting, beautiful and approachable, and designed to be used by the whole family. Your living room is likely located in the most enviable spot in the house, with the best light and the most impressive finishing details, so it should be appreciated and enjoyed every day. Instead of a room that is fancy and off-limits, my goal is to create rooms that are perfectly aligned with your lifestyle and how you live at home, so you can spend time in the best room of the house, surrounded by your favourite things, and the people who matter most.

___

ROSY-HUED REFINEMENT

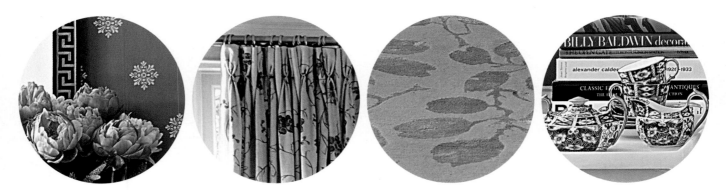

It's not always the biggest rooms that make the best impression or offer the maximum enjoyment factor. Filled with sunlight and infused with a cozy ambiance, this living room has everything one could want in a city home, all tucked into a fairly compact floor plan. With little room for improvement, this space was the only room in the house to survive a dramatic basement-to-rafters renovation with only minor improvements and finishing touches.

PLAY TRICKS ←

At first glance, this room appears saturated with a healthy dose of colour. Touches of pomegranate and coral are sprinkled throughout the room, making it feel alive with rosy hues. But look a little closer, and you'll notice that the more permanent elements in the room, such as the carpet, sofa, walls, chairs, and tables, are all neutrally rooted. The notes of colour that attract your attention are actually just small accents that are by no means permanent. Despite their diminutive size, flowers, books, vases, and pillows used in combination can make a mighty colour impression.

SET YOUR FOCUS ←

An accent wall is hardly a novel idea, but instead of limiting your use of a commanding hit of colour to what comes out of a can, consider what can be achieved with wallpaper. This living room would be overwhelmed if all the walls were covered in rosy-toned wallpaper with gilded accents, but when limited to the chimney breast, it gives just enough energy and elegance to the room while drawing attention to the crisp white mantel and striking black-and-gold Greek key mirror. Since a strong colour pulls your sight line through the room, the use of this paper actually makes the space feel bigger.

STRIKE A BALANCE ←

You might enjoy the idea of living in a century-old home within a historic neighbourhood, though you may not want to make a similar style statement with your decor. The fact that your home was built last century should not preclude you from outfitting it in a way that represents how you live today. Mixing tradition with modernism is an effective way to update your home without stripping out all the character from your surroundings. For best results, select upholstered furnishings that have a clean, streamlined profile and a classic unadorned silhouette. The lean Parsons-style sofa, striped chairs, and subtly patterned, neutral carpet are well-suited partners to the minimal, modern chrome-and-glass coffee table, accent tables, and midcentury chrome chairs.

PLUM PARLOUR

Everyone has a personal sense of style, and knowing what it is will help you make the most of your home and every dollar you spend. I need to live in rooms that are designed for entertaining in sophisticated elegance. I encourage you to design for how you want to live and not defer to an overly casual, dressed-down mood in the principal rooms. Since the living room is supposed to be a sort of salon for receiving guests, it needs to feel properly appointed. I'm not into fussy and off-limits, or fabrics that can't stand up to family life, but a little polish and a nod to glamour is always in the cards when I'm designing!

PLAN FOR CHANGE ➤➤
Allowing your interiors to be influenced by fashion is exciting, but I recommend approaching trends in a flexible way. Instead of making a long-term commitment to a lavender sofa, opt instead for an easy-to-change solution by painting your walls whatever colour of the rainbow tickles your fancy. You can always change the colour of your walls in a weekend on your own, but you probably can't reupholster your sofa (and if you can . . . I'm impressed!).

LOOSEN UP ➤➤
A polished and pretty living room needs a bit of contrast, so add a simple, light textural note with inexpensive sea grass. If you need a palace-sized carpet (this one was 9 feet by 23 feet), it never hurts to choose a stylish and chic floor covering that comes at a reasonable price and can be bound to suit your measurements.

MIX YOUR METALS ➤➤
You don't need to choose cool *or* warm metals — you can have both! My rule for mixing metals is that you need repetition and should use both more than once so it doesn't look like an accent. It works best to also incorporate some items that feature both silver and brass (the wall sconces, coffee table, and drapery hardware are all a combination of both tones).

STRIPE IT UP ➤➤
If you can't find the fabric you want, make it yourself! I bought natural and cream linen, then had them sewn together to create a wide-striped band that runs vertically down the centre of cream-painted vintage chairs and gives a graphic update to a traditional frame.

CHOOSE READY-TO-WEAR ✓
In the past, your only option for ready-made drapes was more collegiate basic than couture. Now, you can buy well-constructed, luxurious interlined drapes that are ready to hang in time for tomorrow's dinner party. Before you assume everything in your living room needs to be bespoke, let your fingers take you on an online adventure, and see what's waiting to be discovered.

TURN THE LIGHTS DOWN ✓
Living rooms tend to be used most in the evening hours, so there's no need to light them up like stadiums. Install pot lights only where you need them to accent a piece of artwork or to light up a dark corner, then use decorative pendant lights and practical table and floor lamps to create mood and ambiance.

SPLIT THE SPACE ↕

Make the best use of a large room by creating distinct areas, zones, or furniture groupings. With two distinct arrangements in a large room, you can have a different experience depending on where you sit. Forget one big grouping filled with overscaled pieces, and make a plan to divide and conquer!

IF YOU DON'T HAVE PEDIGREE, BUY IT! ↕

The best part of buying vintage, beyond the obvious price advantage, is that preloved items have a history. The high-backed chairs were originally purchased for a Spanish embassy in the '50s. Bought and reupholstered for less than you'd pay for new ones, they're not only a good deal but tell a good story.

GET DRAWN IN ←

A mirror is a common decor solution above the fireplace, but if it doesn't reflect an interesting or intriguing vista, it's a missed opportunity; whereas a dynamic and detailed piece of art can catch the eye and grab your attention. This photograph of rooftops in Buenos Aires gives an interesting perspective, and since the mantel is shallow and not too tall, you can get up close and admire it in detail.

BORROW FROM THE PAST ←

Add instant heritage to a brand-new home with salvaged architectural elements, such as a fireplace mantel. You'll need to know the outside width and height of your fireplace opening so you can ensure your new/old mantel is the appropriate size, so measure it up before you shop.

PRETTY PREWAR PARLOUR

Like individuals, some rooms are blessed with character and personality in spades. Imagine how lovely it would be to have your living room perched four floors above street level with views onto a garden below through a leafy canopy of trees. If that sort of outlook isn't compelling enough to make you swoon, sprinkle in a mirror-image pair of fireplaces at both ends of the room and ample square footage, and you'll know why my client wanted to call this international abode home.

BACK IT UP ➥
It's a rare room that offers proportions so perfectly symmetrical that you can create mirror-image groupings within it, but that's exactly what this room seemed to call out for. When setting sofas back-to-back, call attention to your twice-as-nice plan by selecting models with graceful lines and slim, sculptural frames so they don't appear as a weighty mass in the middle of the room. A tight, skinny back with shapely outline was paired with a plush pillow back to afford luxe and loungey comfort within a prim and proper frame. Skip the skirt and opt for a classic turned leg with a brass caster to give the sofa a little levity and keep it from feeling glued to the floor.

MAKE A PERFECT PAIR ➥
I have an affinity for semi-antique Persian carpets and use them as the base of a room whenever the budget and style direction allow. I am also always on the lookout for vintage and antique mirrors. When you're in the mood to hunt for all things vintage and antique, you'll need to remember that pairs are extremely rare. If you need two of something, I suggest you think of your shopping adventure as being akin to seeking spouses, not identical twins — the perfect pairs of mirrors and carpets in this room were kindred spirits with similar palettes and characteristics, yet each is a bit different.

SCULPT IT ↗
Swags, jabots, pelmets, and valances were once common practice in window treatments, but have given way to a simpler style of adorning our windows and framing our views onto the world. If the mood of your room is more stately than subtle, consider amping up the formal factor with a structured, upholstered valance. If mounted flush to the ceiling, your valances needn't limit the light coming into the room, but they will frame the windows and create a continuous floor-to-ceiling show of the beautiful fabric you've selected to dress your windows. The frame of a valance is cut out of wood, so you can custom-design the profile to suit your style (and if you look closely, you'll notice the design here echoes the shapely profile of the sofa backs).

TAKE A LOAD OFF ⬍

Even the most elegant environs need to be able to lighten up and exude a welcoming invitation to kick back and relax. I don't believe in rooms that are off-limits, and I strive to create interiors that will be used and enjoyed each and every day. When my client indicated that she would love to be able to sit and indulge in a cup of tea and read a book in the living room, I knew just what was needed. Dressed in plush mohair velvet, this bold red chaise tucks into a nook beside the fireplace to provide a cozy spot to enjoy the afternoon sun (and perhaps the occasional catnap).

GO TREASURE HUNTING ⟵

After establishing the colour palette for a room, seeking out the finishing touches can be a fruitful and fun adventure if you set your sights on vintage accoutrements with patina and history. With a palette of ruby reds and golds in mind, I turned a small, vintage ice bucket into a cachepot for an orchid, found brass-based hurricane candles, an antique set of etched claret glasses, and even an antique pair of candle sconces, which were wired into electrified wall sconces, for less than I could have paid for any of these items if they were new.

STRIKE A POSE ⟵

Having a variety of seating options within your living room is wise when all the personalities in your home prefer a different option. With plenty of choices to satiate the need for everyday comfort, you can add an upright silhouette to the mix and cover it in a statement fabric for a striking vignette. These gilded Louis XVI-style bergères are framed against a wall of bookshelves with a table to make it easy to leaf through books and reference materials. Since they are light and easy to move, they're intended to float between the reading area where they sit and the adjacent lounge for fireside enjoyment, and they even rate remarkably high in the comfort department despite their posh pedigree.

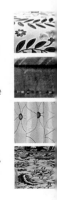

COMPACT CITY CONDO

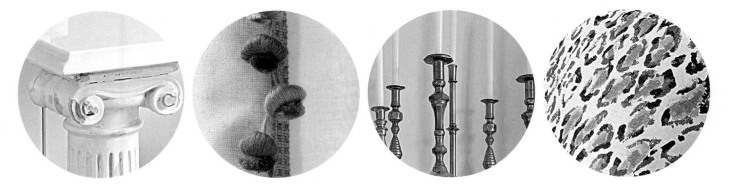

Tiny living spaces have become standard fare for thousands of city dwellers who value their downtown urban lifestyle and would rather live small than spend a hefty percentage of their precious time commuting from the suburbs. If moving to the beat of an urban groove and living in the heart of the action is what matters to you, this pint-sized palace proves that you can squeeze a lot into a little urban oasis.

OVERALL ←↠

Think tall when you're working with small. Making a little room look and live bigger than its pip-squeak proportions is all about tricking the eye and maximizing what you've got to work with. Emphasizing the vertical proportions of the room with streamlined furnishings that are tailored, trim, and tall allows you to squeeze in more furniture without making it feel cramped. Full-height drapes, tall lamps, skinny side tables, and an oversized antique mirror all contribute to the lean, elegant effect of the room.

WALL UNIT ←

Investing in customized solutions allows you to get the most out of every inch. A well-planned built-in can help you achieve a number of goals by combining various functions. The floor-to-ceiling tower conceals a bulkhead while also offering lots of shelves for books and treasures, and the lower section combines the functions of a console, stereo cabinet, and desk/dining table for two. To top it off, the floating shelf alludes to the concept of a fireplace mantel with a place to display candles and artwork above table height to minimize clutter.

COFFEE TABLE ↕

A glass-topped coffee table is a practical solution in a small space. The clear top won't obstruct sight lines, so it seems light and unobtrusive, while the glass surface is durable and easy to care for. A glass coffee table looks best if it's clean and uncluttered, so look out for side tables with drawers and a shelf to give you handy spots for storage.

CONSOLE TABLE AND MIRROR ↕

Small spaces don't usually have a foyer, or even a vestibule, but that doesn't mean you can't create one with clever small-space solutions. A shallow wall-mount iron console and a pretty mirror introduce the illusion of extra space while offering the all-important key and mail depository just inside the door. Since the goal is to make the smallest spaces live larger, another mirror creates additional views both into and out of the space by reflecting the reflection in the living room mirror beyond.

DRAPERY DETAILS ↖

While condos are often geared toward modern minimalism, you can infuse a delicate passementerie to add a flourish of detail. Onion fringe sewn onto the leading edge of your drapes creates a look that's reminiscent of a pretty pied-à-terre, offers the opportunity to reinforce your chosen colour palette, and ups the ante on your window dressing.

MODERN CLASSIC

What's your style? Are you a dyed-in-the-wool traditionalist, a minimal modernist, or a contemporary curator of a little bit of both? The rooms and homes that ignite my creative passion are often a modern-life mix where the architecture serves as a foundation and the interiors are crafted to embrace elegant, original details and sleek contemporary influences in equal measure. In a century-old home, the design brief was to honour the character details while ushering in a modern spirit.

BUILD A FOUNDATION ⊷

If your aesthetic veers to the light and neutral palette of cream, pearl, platinum, oyster, and ecru, you need never worry about taking a major decorating misstep with traumatic results. Tailored furnishings, upholstered in a restrained palette, have proven trend-resistant staying power. When you lay the groundwork by investing in timeless, neutral pieces, you've taken the first step toward longevity, but you've also opened the door to changeability by allowing the flexibility to rethink accents, accessories, and art in the future. With your neutral backdrop, it's always easy to swap out high-impact accents for a new palette and make it look as though you got a whole new room.

BE INSPIRED ⊷

Once you've got a neutral starting point, it's time to turn up the dial and have some fun. Using a painting to help inspire the selection of colours in a room will allow you to highlight the unique palette of colours that the artist chose to include in the work and will likely produce a combination that is unexpected and fresh as opposed to trendy and ubiquitous. Wondering where to start? Since lugging your painting to the fabric store might be tricky, match individual paint chips to all of the colours you like in the painting, and tuck them into an envelope so you can have a quick reference when shopping for matching fabrics and accessories. This approach will let you have fun treating the finishing touches in your room as painterly accents that add a dash of excitement here and a wash of colour there.

MAKE THE MOST OF YOUR ASSETS ↞

Having a home with unusual architectural details is a blessing, but can make the selection of furniture a bit more challenging than shopping for a rectangular box of a room. An offset bay window brings in lovely natural light, though it also makes the placement of a standard-sized sofa look awkward in the room. Instead of crowding the wrong pieces into the space, be realistic about how you are likely to use your living room. Two groupings with more individual chairs may actually be better suited to entertaining—and if you don't have a TV in the room, a full-length sofa may not be necessary.

EDIT YOUR STATEMENT ↞

When it comes to dressing the mantel, I believe less is always more. Presenting a strong, well-edited vignette of beautiful objects on one side of the mantel creates a more stunning visual than little bits and bobs that stretch from side to side and fill the entire space. Since your mantel is likely shallow, look for objects in varying heights with sculptural shapes that aren't too wide in diameter. Uneven groupings always look best, so plan for 3, 5, or 7 pieces in your collection.

GIVE UP COFFEE ↞

A coffee table is a common anchor in a living room furniture grouping that provides a central position around which the furniture is symmetrically arranged. If your living room plan takes a more asymmetrical form, don't feel obliged to try to make a sizable coffee table fit into your space. If flexibility is a priority, you might prefer a collection of occasional tables and footstools, which can be pulled up close to a chair to offer a spot to set down your drink, rearranged to provide extra seating, or used to support tired tootsies. As long as every seat has a table surface within reach from a seated position, you're in good shape.

HALCYON HAVEN

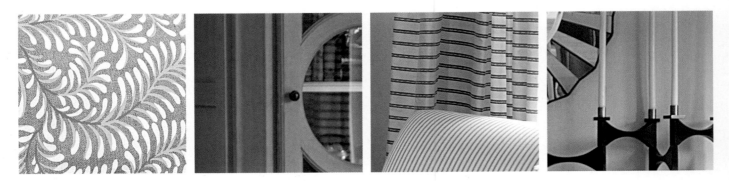

Like people, every room has a distinct personality. Some seem proper and formal and perhaps even a touch intimidating, while others exude friendly warmth and instantly make you feel relaxed. The undeniable first impression of a room can be credited to a sum of its parts, as architecture and decoration blend seamlessly to project a lasting visual impression, and in the case of this home the resulting personality, while elegant and sophisticated, is undeniably friendly and easy to live with.

BRING THE OUTDOORS IN ↗

An exterior copper lantern with seeded glass resembles an old ship lantern and acts as a subtle reference to this home's seaside location. The small bubbles in the glass (which create the seeded effect) cast a dappled shadow pattern on the ceiling. When you install a commanding fixture, it draws the eye up to accentuate the height while also adding a romantic evening ambiance when dimmed low.

GET CLOSE ↗

Many homeowners think their most "important" piece of art should be hung above the living room fireplace in a place of honour; however, I like to consider the height of the mantel before arbitrarily placing it. Art is best when viewed at eye level (and the gallery standard is to hang it so that the centre of the painting is 54 inches above the floor). Keeping your art at a lower level will enable you to get up close and appreciate all the fine details.

MATERIAL MATTERS ↦

When selecting fabric schemes, I prefer to use light, creamy tones for the upholstery and accent with patterned textiles. If you grow tired of the patterns it's easy and inexpensive to introduce an entirely new colour to the room—and everything goes with cream, so you won't need to change the sofa fabric as often as you swap out accessories and finishing touches.

TAKE IT UP A NOTCH ←←

Mattress ticking is a workhorse fabric staple that actually used to be designated to cover a mattress. Tightly woven in 100 percent cotton, this basic is durable and inexpensive and can surpass its humble beginnings to look chic and tailored when used for upholstery on a streamlined silhouette. The mix of formal and informal elements in a room creates spaces that are casually elegant and well suited to modern living.

ADD DRAMA ↘

There are many ways to play with proportion and encourage the eye to travel around the room to absorb all the details. When trying to decide how best to fill the spaces flanking the fireplace, I opted to use a pair of tall and lean cabinets instead of built-in bookshelves. The charcoal-grey finish echoes the smoky palette in the paintings and fabrics, and the freestanding cabinets are a handsome alternative to standard shelves (with the added bonus of being able to move to another rcom, or home, if the need arises).

CONTRASTING DETAILS ↕

Dress up an occasional chair by using a contrasting piping fabric. I find the rich texture of velvet too bulky to be used as piping and often choose a thinner cotton, such as this ticking stripe, to keep the lines of a curvaceous chair looking tailored and elegant.

THE
DINING
ROOM

With frantic schedules and harried households, the stand-alone "formal" dining room runs the risk of becoming completely obsolete in many homes, often replaced by grab 'n' go meals and quick dinners at the kitchen table or in the family room. But I'm a firm believer in the benefits of a proper place to dine. When you gather around a table and share a meal unplugged from work and technology, you have the opportunity to connect with family and friends, engage in dialogue, and celebrate milestones big and small. I am drawn to dining rooms that delight and surprise and encourage everyone to have to good time. So, before you deem the dining room obsolete, I suggest you round up a group, chef up a feast, uncork a bottle (or two), and let the good times roll.

———

BLUE-PLATE SPECIAL

With an overall move toward more casual family living, many families have de-emphasized the importance of a stand-alone dining room in favour of more casual everyday gathering spaces, such as an eat-in kitchen. If the floor plan allows it, I always prefer a separate dining room. I subscribe to an "if you build it, they will come" approach to design and believe in setting the stage by creating rooms that encourage celebrating and entertaining. By rearranging the floor plan of a new-build subdivision home, I created a distinct dining room within an open concept main floor.

——————

MOODY BLUES ➻

Red may be the go-to hue for those in search of a dramatic dining room colour, but I far prefer the cool contrast of rich blues against warm wood furniture. You don't need to limit yourself to one true blue shade—I used denim-blue grasscloth above a chair rail and teal paint below to add both texture and impact. Since the lower section of the wall is more likely to get bumped and scraped, I prefer to apply wallpaper or grasscloth to the upper section, where it can be admired at eye level.

DIVINELY DECO ➻

If your goal is to blend classical beauty with a more contemporary line, you'll likely appreciate the look of vintage Art Deco furniture. With curved doors, a two-tier top, and ample storage, this walnut beauty can hold all the china and crystal you could possibly want or need.

AMP UP THE DETAILS ←

Lots of new-build homes are seriously lacking in architectural interest, but that's an easy fix. Custom-plaster crown moulding can be installed in a day and instantly adds the character befitting a formal dining room.

INVITE AN UNEXPECTED GUEST ←

Artwork should engage and intrigue and help set the mood for the room. This resin-coated photo of a thoroughbred adds an unexpected twist and creates an energy that's more playful than predictably traditional. If you want to create memorable and unique spaces, dare to be different.

EASY AS 1, 2, 3 ←

Instead of using a single upholstery fabric for your chairs, make a multi-textile mix. Mohair velvet seats are super durable (this is what was traditionally chosen for movie theatre seats due to its hardwearing nature), a linen inside back panel has a smoother and more casual feel, and jaunty wide-striped cotton piping and backs helps reinforce the nautically inspired colour palette.

BRASS IS BACK ↘
Dive into your closets and dig out some old treasures, because golden metals are everywhere in design. From trays to candlesticks, sconces to chandeliers, there's a brassy tone on the rise. Look for vintage trays and candlesticks at consignment shops and flea markets, and you'll be able to accessorize your table for a bargain.

GET VINTAGE INSPIRATION ↑
The direction for the colour scheme of a room can come from anywhere — this one originated with a set of vintage dishes I discovered in a consignment shop. Once you've got a basic set of china, you can add boldly patterned salad plates and serving pieces to your settings for a modern mix.

WOODLAND DELIGHT

When embarking on any new design project, I think of the house as a whole unit, and each room as an opportunity to explore new ideas while maintaining a consistent and cohesive point of view and plan. My theory is that each room should make a unique visual statement, yet feel sympathetic and complementary to the adjoining spaces. In essence it leads me to experiment with different combinations in each space designed to service a different purpose; the result is a home that flows from one room to the next while offering unexpected combinations and engaging environments. In a Tudor-style home, I called on Arts and Crafts inspiration as the springboard for a warm and welcoming dining room.

TAKE IT TO THE TOP ←

To give a dark dining room updated polish, take a departure from stained-wood panelling and paint it a light, bright white. This may be a controversial suggestion to some, but using the panelling as a high-contrast background to antique wood furnishings allows the decorative details of the furniture to shine. To amp up the drama, select a bold wallpaper to create moody nighttime ambiance and apply it to the upper section of the walls. Don't overlook the ceiling—pulling the colour out of the rug and applying it to the ceiling draws the eye up and accentuates the beautiful crown moulding.

CREATE A MELTING POT ←

Contemporary design offers the opportunity to combine elements from around the globe and curate rooms that are as eclectic and adventurous as you dare. If you want to live in dynamic rooms, consider taking an international approach to your selections. The table and wallpaper are English designs, the chairs are a French reproduction, the chandelier is vintage Italian, and the carpet is a contemporary interpretation of the acanthus-leaf motif popular in ancient Greece (but woven in Nepal). There's no need to follow a strictly homegrown approach to style when you can take a world tour!

A DASH WILL DO →
Designing within a framework of traditional style without making your rooms appear stuffy and staid relies on the mix of ingredients. Embracing historical elements, and combining them with contemporary influences, will enable you to create a home that draws inspiration from classic references while keeping in step with modern living. If combined strictly with Arts and Crafts elements, the William Morris wallpaper from the 1800s might seem like a dour time capsule, but when paired in equal measure with restrained fabrics and a contemporary carpet, the wallpaper reads as a richly patterned accent in a tailored environment.

FLOWERS →
For a foolproof way to arrange flowers and look like a pro, try selecting a single variety of blooms (with no greenery), cut them all the same length, and cluster them together in a clear glass vase with simple lines. If you want to make a larger statement, create a cluster of vases, each filled with a different variety and colour of blooms with staggered heights. Bold colours can add a pop of pizzazz to reinforce an accent colour in your walls or carpet.

DOUBLE OR NOTHING →
Love two fabrics for your dining chairs but can't decide which one to choose? Why not use both? You can add extra interest to upholstered chairs by covering the seat and the inside back in one fabric and using a stronger accent fabric on the outside back. The simple stripe pulls in a few colours from the wallpaper and acts as a contrast to the busy pattern.

DECO DINING LOUNGE

Many houses built in the late 1880s and early 1900s are located in the best neighbourhoods of major cities and are therefore in high demand. Built to last and filled with charm, these old houses often featured a segregated floor plan, which many homeowners who crave an open-concept floor plan that's more in line with their contemporary lifestyle consider a negative. For a couple downsizing from a larger family home, the goal was to create an open-concept dining room that still retained a level of sophistication without feeling off-limits for more casual family gatherings.

GO BIG FOR SMALL ⇢
When you've got a petite, open-concept dining area, there's limited opportunity to make a statement, since you'll only have a few pieces of furniture. So I often rely on fabrics to introduce texture and softness. Upholstered dining chairs provide comfortable seating with a less formal feel, and you'll need less than two yards of fabric per chair, which makes your dining chairs an ideal place to experiment with a bold gesture. Instead of a solid or a mini print, I gravitate toward larger-scaled prints even on small upholstered pieces. This bird-silhouette print is well suited to the garden views in this room, and the monochromatic palette isn't overpowering.

CREATE A BACKDROP ⇢
With few walls and no doors in your open-concept dining area, defining the space and setting the scene can be challenging. Grasscloth wallpaper, installed along the length of the room from floor to ceiling, acts as a backdrop for a gallery wall of sketches in gilded frames. With no trim details to cap the end of the walls, carrying the grasscloth throughout the room might have proved an impractical choice for wear and tear, as it would get dinged on outside corners and appear tattered. Limiting the install to a single wall with inside corners is a surefire way to keep your decorative wallcoverings looking their best for the long haul.

PICTURE PERFECT ⇢
When hanging a collection of artwork, it's easy to present a unified front by allowing the same spacing between each print. A safe rule of thumb is about 3 to 4 inches between and above every piece. Keep it consistent and you'll look like a pro! If you find that you are working with a number of frames with different proportions, you may find it best to set them all to a centre line. Keep the bottoms of the top row and the tops of the bottom row at the same heights, and then hang a single piece on the ends that is centred on the spacing. Just remember to measure at least twice before you hammer!

LOOK DOWN ↧
Deciding on jumping-off points can be challenging, especially if you are starting with a blank slate. Finding the right carpet in a size and style that fits the room at a price that suits your budget can be like looking for the proverbial needle in a haystack. It will likely be easier to find fabrics that complement your carpet rather than the other way around, so consider building your room from the ground up. This Tabriz carpet is ideally suited to a dining room due to its tightly knotted construction, which creates a dense and durable layer underfoot. The overall pattern is forgiving when spills occur, and the pale neutral palette, with touches of soft blues and greens, draws out accent colours for both the dining room and the adjacent kitchen area.

LAVISH DINING SUITE

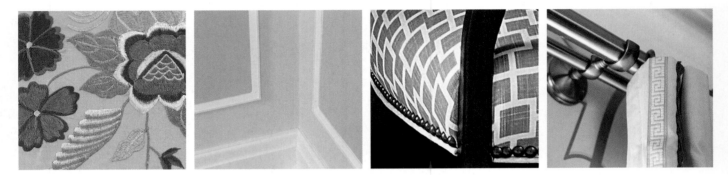

I like to think of the formal dining room as a special place where good times are had, milestones are celebrated, and occasions are marked in the collective family history. If you've got a stand-alone dining room that is divided from the rest of the home, let's talk about what you can do to turn that dinosaur into a dynamite destination!

MAKE A STATEMENT ⇢

When a room lacks personality and architectural features, you can start by amping up the appeal factor of the basic box. It doesn't need to be expensive or extravagant, but you may find that a simple addition of trim details creates a more formal look. Taking cues from the existing plaster crown moulding, I selected a chair rail and panel profile to be installed on the lower portion of all the walls, enabling us to apply a three-colour paint scheme. Chair rail is usually installed from 24 to 36 inches above the floor; however, you can select your own height to suit your purposes. I opted to install the rail at 42 inches so it would not interfere with the height of the sideboard.

PASS ON THE SUITES ⇢

If you're starting out and furnishing your home for the long haul, it makes sense to buy the best you can afford. It's easy to buy a suite of furniture comprising matching chairs, sideboard, and table, but it devalues and is worth a fraction of the sticker price once you've paid and it crosses your threshold, so I've always been an advocate of seeking out vintage or, better yet, antique pieces, which, if bought well, will retain their value or even appreciate as time marches on. A dining table with exceptionally beautiful wood grain on the top, and a complementary (but not matching) Sheraton-style sideboard, are more dynamic and more interesting to look at than any new suite, and they infuse a soulful, traditional spirit to what was once a lacklustre room.

HAVE A SEAT ⇢

Since there aren't many places to make a statement in a small dining room, I'm always on the lookout for chairs that combine comfort and elegance with shapely lines for visual interest. This set of 6 shield-back chairs with vintage pedigree and great lines at a bargain price fit the bill perfectly. If you're willing to look past the existing upholstery and spend some energy getting vintage chairs refinished, you'll be sitting pretty with chairs that have character and personality.

ADD A GRAPHIC TOUCH ⇢

With the goal of lightening, brightening, and invigorating this little room and turning it into a jewel box of sorts, the main upholstery fabric (a mustard-toned geometric on a cotton ground) is a dramatic departure from the floral silk. The yellow appears in the embroidered fabric, offers the opportunity to make a youthful and cheery statement, and is easy-care cotton that's also easy on the budget.

LEAD WITH LUXURY ⇢

A bland room with lacklustre appeal needs pizzazz and texture, something that feels fancy and exuberant. I've always appreciated the rich detail of embroidered silk with saturated colours and lyrical patterns offered on a rainbow assortment of backgrounds. Since I'm practical by nature, this would never pass as a main upholstery fabric (plus it tends to be a bit pricey), but it's an interesting and unexpected choice for the outside back of your chairs (which won't fall prey to the same wear and tear as the seats, unless your typical dinner-party fare is wings coated in barbeque sauce).

REPEAT AFTER ME ↕

I like patterns and repetition and have a penchant for repeating motifs. I find that my eye tends to travel around a room, absorbing all the details and looking for linking elements. In this room, the shape of the shield-back chairs works with the linking scroll pattern of the wallpaper, and the painted detail on the floor matches the corner of the mirror (unintentionally, but happily), while also connecting to the Greek key banding on the drapes and the square geometric pattern on the chairs. As I'm someone constantly in search of visual beauty, this repetition satiates my desire for harmony and order.

WORK WITH WHAT YOU'VE GOT ↕

In some cases, the only way to get gleaming hardwood floors is to rip out what you've got and start fresh, but it's not always necessary. If your floorboards are in good condition and only suffer from an unfortunate shade of stain, it's an easy job to sand and refinish your floors for a fraction of the price of installing new. It can be done as a DIY project if you're really handy, or you can leave it to the pros (my mom and I still get the giggles over a memorable refinishing experience many years ago . . .).

GET INSTANT HISTORY ↩

Some of us have china and crystal, silver and linen, in spades, passed down from grandmothers and great-aunts, and some of us don't. The good news is that if your china cabinet isn't over-flowing with an abundance of hand-me-down table settings you adore, you can amass a veritable abundance of exceptional beauty for a pauper's price. The table is set with intricately detailed silver-plate cutlery, vividly hand-painted fine bone china with a funky hot-pink floral border that's anything but fussy, and a whole collection of silver-plate serving pieces and candlesticks starting with single-digit price tags at consignment and pawnshops. If you're looking to outfit your dining room with beautiful goods at bargain prices, buy used, and celebrate the fabulous finds!

PLAYFUL EDWARDIAN

Many of us are drawn to old houses for their original charm and graceful proportions. But sometimes, the heavy finishes and traditional features are at odds with the youthful family spirit that occupies the home. This is when a rethink is needed. Keeping the character and breathing new life into a drab and dated space with paint, fabric, and imagination showcases the power of decorating to redefine rooms without making structural changes. This dining room is proof positive that any old room can lighten up and brighten up to make everyday living feel like a celebration.

CREATE HARMONY ↣

Repainting wood chairs and a sideboard in glossy black infuses tension into the room, provides contrast to the light walls and tables, and ties in the line drawings on the drapes and the painted details on the windows and doors. Painting furniture is also a handy way to unify varying wood finishes to create a more cohesive palette. Crisp black and white always looks right!

BE PRACTICALLY STYLISH ↣

If the mandate is family-friendly dining, you'll need surfaces that withstand the wear and tear of the under-five set. A vintage '70s laminate table brings authentic style in the form of a simple Parsons design (and the bargain price makes it easy for any budget to swallow). Thanks to the timeless lines, it can be dressed up with fine china and elegant touches for entertaining or be enjoyed for daily dining and scrubbed clean after the meal is done.

ADD SOME POLISH ↗

Choose a chandelier and wall sconces in a shiny chrome finish to bring a bright touch of Hollywood Regency shine to your space. Streamlined crystals reflect and add a hint of formal elegance, while bright white metal makes sure the mood is anything but fussy.

EMBRACE THE OPTIONS ↣

Why choose option A, B, C, or D when you can play multiple choice and have all of the above? Instead of committing to a single colour for upholstery, match all the colours in your patterned fabric and take a multihued approach to your dining chairs. Upholster a set of 8 in 4 bright, bold colours and you'll have snappy mix-n-match style. If you want your chairs to be virtually indestructible, choose outdoor fabric for the upholstery and you won't cringe when the kids dive into chocolate cake for dessert. It's durable, scrubbable, and means you can have upholstery without the worry!

HIGHLIGHT YOUR FEATURES ↠

Instead of transitioning from dark up to light, turn your colour upside down. When you treat the space above the plate rail to a strong shade, such as this blue, it draws the focus upwards, accentuates the high ceilings, and keeps the lower portion of the room bright and airy. Add an instant update to a dowdy-looking room by painting the woodwork in a light, silvery tone, and extend the view by highlighting the window frames and recessed panels on the doors with black paint to draw the focus out and pull the sight lines through the space.

GO GROOVY ↕

Don't play it safe and serious—inject some fun into your dining room by using a lighthearted and energetic fabric. Embroidered street scenes of line-drawn people have an urban graffiti edge that appeals to the younger set and is well suited to a room that's supposed to encourage spirit and frivolity.

THE LIVING/ DINING ROOM

Joining forces and combining your living room and dining room into one open-concept space gives you the best of both worlds by allowing you to be in both rooms at once. By knocking out walls and making two into one, you'll benefit from a feeling of more space and more flexibility around how you prioritize and delineate the eating and lounging functions in your home. As someone who endeavours to make every space live as large as possible, I am drawn to the "bigger is better" result of open-concept spaces. If you live a modern lifestyle and take a laid-back approach to entertaining, I suggest you break down the walls and make the most of what you've got.

MIDCENTURY MASTERPIECE

There is no such thing as a perfect house. Getting the home of your dreams requires time and effort to create a space that is uniquely you. If you are prepared to tackle a challenge, you will likely be rewarded with exciting possibilities to tweak and remodel your new home to suit your style. Instead of buying a small unit in a newly erected condominium, my client opted to take a chance on a dated '80s condo to score more square footage and a prime address. My job was to make it light and bright and open, with a mix of contemporary design and modern classic furnishings.

DRAW IT OUT ↤
Inspiration for a design scheme can come from anywhere. For this sky-high condo, the blue notes were drawn from the artwork and then repeated on accent chairs, dining chairs, and accessories. If you are wondering where to start your design journey, pull out your favourite pieces of art and see which colours are most appealing to you.

PICK A GOOD VINTAGE ↤
When you're looking to get the most for the least, just remember that secondhand furnishings can usually be found at more reasonable prices than new pieces of comparable value. Vintage goods are often better quality and add character and charm to your home. My favourite pieces in any room I design are always the vintage finds. From garage sales to estate sales to auction houses to antique stores, I'm always looking for vintage treasures.

MAKE SCULPTURAL SELECTIONS ↕

When working within the confines of a small space, every piece you buy matters, so try to incorporate elements with interesting lines and sculptural appeal. A vintage pair of chrome office chairs has compact proportions well suited to a small city condo and can be swivelled to follow the action whether it's in the dining or living area. The wishbone shape of the bases and the sinuous arm profile make their presence notable yet unobtrusive. The exaggerated tapered legs made of horns on the tripod table appear to be floating delicately in the room and ground the interior with a natural element.

BE CONSISTENT ↕

You may be using a number of pieces from different sources, and different design periods, to cultivate your signature curated collection, but the key to creating a cohesive interior is using similar fabrics and wood tones. This will im-mediately create a more cohesive look in your home, so treat an open-concept space to the same scheme throughout all the areas. To create this modern mix, charcoal, cream, sapphire, and persimmon are peppered throughout the living area with midtone woods and chrome accents. If you want to add a current trend element to your rooms, do it in small doses that are easy to change in the future. Pillows and accessories can help you achieve an up-to-the-minute look that you won't be stuck with forever. I'm always game for a hint of animal print in pillows, but my need for timeless style choices guides me to take a pass on an entire sofa in orange zebra. Moderation is the key to being fashion forward at home.

TOP IT UP ⇡
Buying vintage doesn't dictate using the pieces you find "as is."
While on the hunt for a simple, modern coffee table, I discovered an
inexpensive solid-wood Parsons table that I had stripped and refinished
and then topped with a new marble tabletop cut to fit the exact dimensions
of the table with no overhang. The grey-veined Carrara marble adds
a durable surface to the table, while lightening up the room.

BE OPEN TO THE POWER OF SUGGESTION ⇡
Having a set shopping list in mind when sourcing new items is an achievable
goal; however, if a vintage mix is what you're after, you'll need to allow yourself
to be inspired by what you find in your travels. To outfit this compact sunroom,
I knew I wanted a pair of chairs with both character and comfort in spades, but
these criteria come in many shapes and sizes. You may need to look beyond
some pretty-dated upholstery fabric (such as the original brown plaid on these
'70s teak numbers), but if you can imagine them transformed
by reupholstery, you'll be able to score a winning solution.

KEEP IT LIGHT ↤
Small spaces can quickly feel crowded with too much furniture, but a clear glass coffee table with a fluid waterfall edge allows you to see right through and keeps the main lounge area feeling open and uncluttered, while also enabling a better view of the cowhide floor covering. The rounded profile of the coffee table is echoed in the vintage Art Deco buffet, which was turned into a much-needed storage piece, since condominiums are notoriously short on spots to stash all your stuff. You might not think to bring a touch of Deco to your modern mix, but with such simple lines and striking chrome and black hardware, it makes a good complement to the midcentury pieces.

USE SPARINGLY ↤
Accent colours are intended to add impact and excitement to a room, not overpower it, so be judicious with how and where you inject colour. After the furnishing and decorating of the entire space, the living room was still missing something, so I bought a quart of blue paint and wrapped it around two small wall sections to create an enticing focal point in the far corner of the living room. When painting walls in a dramatic shade, opt for a flat finish paint so the end result looks rich and velvety. A flat finish paint will also help disguise a less than flawless finish if you're doing it yourself, as sheen shows every brushstroke.

SILVER SCREEN SALON

While most clients place the desire for a family room near the top of their wish list for functional rooms on the main floor, not everyone sees it the same way. For a pair of stylish, luxury-loving empty nesters, the brief was to design a living/dining room space with a few ground rules: seating for six; a place for morning coffee, newspaper reading, and news watching; and a place to sit comfortably to connect with each other.

MIX AND MATCH ➼

Every family room needs comfortable lounge seating, but there's no rule dictating that they must match. Two distinct chairs can be unified to work as a his-and-hers pairing by upholstering them in the same fabric, with matching wood stain on the leafs. Lean frames and elegant silhouettes complement each other while offering two distinctly different options for everyday lounging.

BE TRANSPARENT ➼

With narrow proportions, a room can feel cramped if all the furnishings are solid and bulky, so a low, contemporary glass coffee table with a boxy chrome frame was chosen to reference the light and airy dining table.

TAKE A SEAT ⬆

An upholstered dining chair is often the choice for comfort and softness, but with a large room and the long banquette, something with more sculptural impact was needed. A set of Chippendale-style raw-wood frames from a local chair supplier were sprayed in high-gloss feather-grey lacquer and reupholstered in a retro metallic weave. Reinterpreting styles and patterns allows you to add modern flair to traditional design elements.

PUT IT ON A PEDESTAL ⬆

Once you've committed to a banquette, it limits your table selection, as the traditional four legs make entry and exit reminiscent of a toddler navigating a jungle gym. I found the right balance of translucence, sheen, and rarity in the form of a white lacquered, Deco-inspired pedestal base from the '70s with a thick glass top that sets the tone for chic, modern sophistication.

INVEST IN METALS ↕

A fun way to start formulating a concept for a room that you're starting from
scratch in designing is to agree on a single word that embodies the feel of the
colour, quality, luxury, and elegance of the room. In this case, *platinum* summed
it up well. A precious metal synonymous with luxury and cool elegance became
the directional cue for all ensuing design directions.

NO RESERVATION REQUIRED ↕

Taking a cue from the classic restaurant approach to space-saving seating,
I designed a custom L-shaped banquette that spans the entire length of one
wall—14 feet of silver-celery-toned chenille with a diamond-tufted back. The
custom solution allows more space for the lounge area and allowed the dining
table to tuck into a corner of the banquette to make the best use of space.

ILLUMINATE & DELIGHT ↠
Overhead ceiling pendants can be treated as overall illumination and centred on the overall dimensions of the room, or they can be hung to relate to a specific piece of furniture. In a room with high ceilings and an asymmetrical layout, you may find it more effective to follow the overall illumination route and allow yourself the most flexibility when it comes to furniture placement. No matter where the fixtures are installed, it's important that your lighting be interesting, unusual, and impactful. These pendants, comprising a series of Japanese papers with poems, notes, scribbles, and sketches suspended on a wire-clip frame, certainly generate conversation and elicit a response, but never fade into the background!

BELLE OF THE BALL ↠
Window coverings are an important part of the overall design scheme and should complement the design direction. Since every element in the room was an equal ratio of one part luxe, one part modern, powdery grey-blue silk taffeta drapes befitting a debutante ball were juxtaposed with contemporary stainless-steel hardware for a look that's elegant without being opulent.

DRESS IT UP ↠
Too much upholstery can make a room seem like a poorly orchestrated statement, or a single note lacking variety. To bring unexpected contrast and formal elegance to the mix, a hand-carved Louis XVI-style sofa frame was custom painted to complement the platinum theme. If you're looking to make old-world style pieces look fresh and modern, choose an understated fabric in a neutral tone so the focus is on the shapeliness of the furniture silhouette rather than the fanciful expression of the fabric.

KEEP IT LEAN ↗
Some rooms call for chunky side tables and amply proportioned lamps, but in a room where the goal is to create the best seating arrangements within a compact footprint, some adjustments may need to be made. When a large-scale coffee table is in proximity, you may only need a tiny table to rest your drink, accompanied by a slim and trim candlestick lamp to illuminate what you are reading. High-gloss white lacquer side tables and tall, shiny chrome candlestick lamps with aqua-tinted shades added a few finishing touches of polish and sparkle to the mix.

SIXTIES SIDE-SPLIT

If you've lost that loving feeling with your living spaces, it may be time to reevaluate and take charge. Is the awkward and unusual layout of your room the root of the problem, or are you just not accepting what's unique and potentially interesting and different about the architecture of your home? Sure, it would be easier if you had a straightforward, symmetrical configuration that dictated a simple and standard furniture layout . . . but where's the fun in that? Perhaps the aspects of your room that currently pose the greatest challenge could prove themselves to be an asset if you conquer the floor-plan and find a way to make all the available space work, even if it means creating distinct zones instead of one large seating area.

WHERE TO START ↤

If an awkward floor plan is your current dilemma, my suggestion is to ignore any preconceived notions about how you "should" arrange the room and approach the challenge as if it were a puzzle. Try to ignore the standards of "normal" living room layouts, and you just might arrive at a new idea that works better than you could have imagined, without breaking down walls or reprogramming the house.

GET A PENDANT WITH PIZZAZZ ↤

Lighting can make or break a room, so you should never underestimate its importance. If you're rethinking your dining room configuration and breaking away from the norm, why settle for a classic chandelier? Even a simple and streamlined contemporary light fixture can up the ante in the ambiance department when it has a geometrically patterned, perforated form that casts a pattern of dappled light on the walls and ceiling.

DEEMPHASIZE THE ELEPHANT IN THE ROOM ←

When you've got a home with a challenging and dominating design feature that you don't intend to change, you just need to acknowledge it and embrace it and make it part of the new scheme. The grey brick wall seemed overpowering in the previous incarnation of the room, but by selecting a palette that complements a strong feature, you can turn it to your advantage. Instead of fighting the brick, we treated it as a neutral backdrop and accentuated the area with an interesting slab of stone with dynamic veining that breathed new life and presence into an existing feature.

NATURALLY NEUTRAL — WITH A TWIST ↕

The design direction of this room was focused on layering earthy neutrals to create a tranquil and harmonious setting. But instead of diving into an endless sea of beige, I relied on accents of spruce, olive, ochre, and russet to reference the changing seasonal vistas that serve as the backdrop to this area thanks to large-scale walls of glass. In a midcentury home outfitted with vintage midcentury fittings, a retro-inspired stylized floral seemed perfectly at home as the main pattern attraction. A touch of colour here and a hint of pattern there is all you need to invigorate a naturally neutral environment.

BREAK OLD HABITS ←

The urge to put the sofa opposite the fireplace is a natural reaction, as a sofa seems to be an equal anchor to the mass of the hearth, as well as a cozy place to enjoy the heat in proximity. However, it's possible that allowing the biggest piece of furniture to dominate and dictate where everything else fits in might be the root of the problem. By moving the sofa away from the "main" seating grouping, you'll effectively be able to create two distinct seating areas that are geared towards different experiences and different views within the room. By sliding the sofa away from a giant picture window and back against the far wall, a snug and private lounge area was created and the living room felt as though it were nearly doubled in size.

SMOKE AND MIRRORS ←

Embrace the magic of smoke and mirrors, or better yet . . . smoked mirrors! Often considered dated (and not highly design rated), I think tinted mirrors are making a comeback. When used in a scheme of similar tones, a grey smoked mirror creates a wide interior reflection and offers visual expansion to cramped or awkward areas. Thanks to the magic of mirrors, you can sit and look out the front window of this house while also appreciating the reflected beauty of the garden behind.

RETHINK STANDARD DINING ROOM FARE

We all need storage for china and crystal, platters, and presentation pieces, but there's no mandate dictating a giant, long sideboard and 8 identical chairs in your dining environment. If you gravitate to a more contemporary look, why not consider using a tall vertical storage cabinet as a visual barrier between different zones in an open-concept space, as well as an efficient way to stow as much as possible, as efficiently as possible. If you build tall and skinny combined with long and low (in the form of a custom banquette made from existing pieces), you'll be able to more than double your capacity to stow and stash without cramping your design style. Since standard kitchen cabinet components, which I used, come in a variety of heights, you'll be able to configure them to suit your needs perfectly and even integrate an area for open storage and display.

DON'T BE EXTREME ↘

Just because you want to revamp doesn't mean you have to get rid of *everything*.
Reimagining a favourite preloved sofa, chair, or existing piece of furniture allows
you to breathe new energy into old stuff. If you've got upholstered pieces that are
comfortable with good clean lines, why not give them a new lease on life with a
makeover? Vintage furniture is often better made than what you'll find in a store
today, and the tailored proportions are well suited to a tight space. Plus you just
can't beat the price of stuff you already own — it doesn't get any better than free.

JADE JEWEL BOX

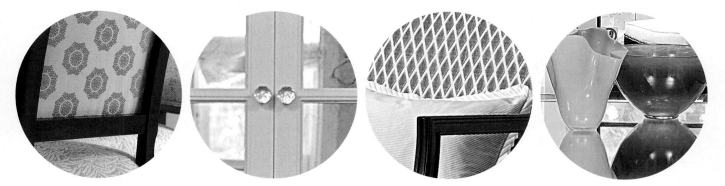

When renovating a house that's over a hundred years old, the style debate revolves around how to revitalize it. Do you strip it back to the structure and finish it with a cool modern mandate, or do you restore the past while updating it with historical architectural details and accents? For this homeowner, the fine balance was achieved through an extensive renovation that embraced traditional ornamentation, and an interior that marries the best of both worlds.

THE CROWNING TOUCH ←
What colour should you paint your crown (or cornice) moulding? The answer is simple: flat pure white to highlight the difference in colour between your walls and ceiling — it looks like solid plaster, which is what crown was typically made of before we had the alternatives of wood and MDF.

GARDEN DELIGHTS ↕

In a classic Victorian home the dining room is situated in the middle of the house and receives limited natural light. To counteract the lack of brightness, I selected a vibrant leafy palette. The grassy green hues are fresh and invigorating, and the unexpected colour lends contemporary flair to the traditional architecture of the house. The woven-leaf pattern on the seats links to the gilded-leaf sconces on the wall, while the bold contemporary painting reinforces the garden theme without looking too stuffy.

FOOLED YOU ↕

To create the illusion of additional windows, the doors of this built-in china cabinet have been fitted with mirrored panels instead of clear glass. A traditional china cupboard seemed too predictable for this renovated row house. Now the mirrors reflect the artwork and the crystal chandelier, and bring a touch of sparkle to this restrained room.

DIVIDE AND CONQUER ←

The long, narrow proportions of a Victorian town house are often best addressed with two distinct seating groupings. When entertaining, it's rare to have all your guests engaged in a single conversation, so you might as well divide the room into intimate groupings that offer the best opportunities for lounging, relaxing, and entertaining, whether it's being used by just one person or a group of eight.

FRAME THE VIEW ←

Give plain old white windows a pass and dress up your window muntins with a coat of high gloss black paint while keeping the frames bright white to create a punch of depth while alluding to the old-world look of leaded glass.

VARIATIONS ON A THEME ←

Take black and white to the max in multiple combinations of the classic yin and yang. Lighten a black granite side table with a polished lamp that visually floats above the chaise, and play with grayscale by introducing black-and-cream-striped accent cushions, chairs, and striped drapes. It's a study in contrasts that's sure to please!

BUTTON UP ←

Buttons are like jewellery when they embellish a pillow. Pay attention to small details that can add a special touch to every element in your room. A bejewelled accent lends a glamourous twist to a Deco-inspired tub chair dressed in an otherwise muted palette of menswear-inspired black and cream.

TROPICAL ADVENTURE ⇡

Looking to add an island influence to your home without making a permanent commitment to life in the southern hemisphere? Play up a tropical twist by adding bold directions in subtle doses. Instead of a giant palm-covered sofa, experiment with large-scale patterns in small accents, and you'll find that they can still make a big statement.

STEP 1,2,3 ⇲

The most memorable interiors are unique and filled with clever ideas. When considering what to hang on your walls, look beyond the basics and stretch your imagination to think about what would make you feel happy to look at every day. This trio of vintage gilded sunburst mirrors adds a playful twist to a sophisticated room and acts as the centre point to a symmetrical seating group that combines an Art Deco table with a vintage black lacquer and gold footstool and a pair of ebonized armchairs dressed in luxurious cut velvet.

LOUNGE LIVING ⇡

Don't be afraid to stray from traditional furniture groupings of sofas, love seats, and chairs. Opt instead for decadent and comfortable pieces that suit your lifestyle. Tucking a cushy chaise into a corner creates an invitation to cozy up and read the paper or a favourite novel, or take a catnap in the afternoon sun. With the long seat cushion, it can be useful as a perch for two people to have a tête-à-tête during your next soirée.

KEEP IT LEAN ⇠

Making any room work is really just about playing with proportions. When you've got a narrow room, the trick is to select shallow and narrow pieces of furniture to achieve your goal. Streamlined chairs and a sofa can still offer great comfort without wasting an inch of circulation space, and you'll be able to find a workable furniture layout with proper flow. For best results, place your sofa and chairs first, and then experiment to see what proportion of table feels most comfortable to you. If possible, bring the table home for a test run and try before you buy!

COOL TOWN HOUSE

I've long been a fan of the century-old classic city row house. In its original form, the "small rooms" plan of a row house can feel tight and cramped; however, after undergoing the transformation of a contemporary reno, these small spaces become light and airy open-concept homes with high ceilings and flexible space. While I'm a fan of the efficiency presented by the row house vernacular, I'm also well versed in the challenges of trying to squeeze all the needs of a family into one room. A modern couple with a toddler called on me to turn a style-challenged blank slate into a crisp and contemporary family living area that could transition from family play zone into adult entertaining environment with a snap.

MAKE A PLAN ➻
The key to decorating success here lies in having a master plan where all the elements work seamlessly together. Any home designed for family living needs to be infused with a healthy dose of practicality, and all decisions need to be made with lifestyle and daily usage in mind. That said, there's absolutely no reason to sacrifice style simply because you have little ones underfoot. I want to have it all and believe you can too!

PICK A COOL NEUTRAL ➻
I'm sure you've heard it said that "grey is the new beige." You can never go too wrong if you work your decor around a tried-and-true natural hue. Instead of simply grey, I've always gravitated to the oyster-toned shades of grey. With a slight hint of green and a touch of sand, the right grey for me is a changeable choice that alters with the light and the time of day. It will never feel too cold, yet it will prove itself to be an adaptable and flexible choice that combines with a wide range of accent colours (which

can be used to add vibrancy and energy to your living quarters). As an added bonus, if you've embraced the warm-hued tones of teak, you'll find the cooler side of grey is a more flattering partner than old-school beige.

BE CLEAR ➻
Adding a glint of light and a hint of sparkle to every room is a habit of mine. In a room predominated by wood and neutral greys, there's still opportunity for some glassy elements in unexpected places. While stainless and black iron may be the common choices for drapery rods, there are alternatives to consider. Since we only had two windows to dress, I opted to pay a little premium to get clear acrylic rods. I know it's a small touch, but in every project it's the details that make the room work!

ALL THAT GLOWS ↕

Even the sleekest, coolest spaces need a touch of texture. I gravitate to the tactile beauty of handmade elements for the unique effect they bring. The crowning touch to a pint-sized dining area needed to have spirit and soul, and that's just what you get from this punctured brass hanging pendant. With a silvered exterior and golden interior, this intricately patterned fixture casts a delicate play of light on the ceiling above and gives the tried-and-true chandelier a run for the money when it comes to chic solutions.

DEMAND DOUBLE DUTY ↕

If you're suffering from the challenge of a living room that is overrun with toys and kid-related paraphernalia, you need to demand more from your furniture choices and embrace every opportunity to stash and stow the necessary trappings and accoutrements that come along with children. When buying side tables, try to find options with an additional shelf, select an entry console that also incorporates closed storage, and seek out innovative 2-in-1 options such as the upholstered stools that double as storage bins. Covered in a practical cotton/linen blend, these affordable ottomans make stashing toys an accessible solution to the clutter conundrum.

START WITH THE CLASSICS ⇡

The best budget-buster advice I have is to buy collectible classic furnishings. While teak furniture was previously viewed as strictly the domain of families with the last name Brady or homes featuring an extensive installation of shag carpeting, teak is no longer a time-warp design. The tailored proportions, clean lines, and restrained forms of vintage pieces are well scaled for small-space living, and teak is proving to be a contemporary classic well suited to life in the 21st century. Often available at bargain prices in vintage and consignment stores, with no need for refinishing, a collection of teak finds kick-started my decorating project with fiscal frugality in mind.

GO FOR WASH 'N' WEAR ⇡

Most of the rooms I've tackled for TV balance a seamless combination of "high" and "low" elements, and this one is no exception. My practical nature demands that upholstery fabrics be chosen with spills and mishaps in mind, so I am a huge fan of durable, washable, inexpensive cotton twill. When disaster inevitably strikes, the covers can simply be zipped off and tossed in the washing machine to return to their "as new" condition. Living rooms shouldn't be off-limits, and washable fabrics ensure that there are no regrets. (I find that covers wash best when there's no piping, and it's always key to prewash and preshrink your fabric *before* you have the sofa made!

MAY I TAKE YOUR ORDER? ↤

With a minuscule dining area that measured less than 9 feet wide (!), the seating options were limited, to say the least, so I finally decided the only route was a custom choice. I looked to restaurant design for a viable solution and borrowed a page from the classic wraparound banquette commonly used to cram maximum guests into minimum space. By tucking an L-shaped banquette into one corner, it eliminated the need for circulation space around the table and enabled me to create a dining destination that's as alluring as the best neighbourhood bistro.

PUT IT ON A PEDESTAL ↤

To get the best functionality out of your dining area, you need to pair your seating with the most appropriate table choice. When using a banquette and attempting to save on circulation space, a pedestal table is a must. Thanks to a single post on a pedestal, everyone can slide in and out without whacking their kneecaps, and no one at the table will be forced to straddle a leg.

SEAM IT UP ↘

The key to flexibility with one long room is the choice of area rug. You can go custom and have a piece of broadloom cut and bound to your specific dimensions, but if you want to dress your floor with a dynamic pattern, you may need a different solution. Area rugs aren't generally offered in proportions that can be likened to a runway, so if the standard 8-by-10-foot or 9-by-12-foot options aren't making the cut, why not make the size you need from what's available? I found a funky 8-by-10-foot, pale grey, zebra-patterned, pure-wool rug and opted to have two of them sewn together along the 10-foot side to create a single 10-by-16-foot carpet that defined the living room. Including the cost to have the rugs sewn together, my total price was still far less than what you'd pay for any "palace-sized" carpet in existence.

INDUSTRIAL LOFT

The concept of living in a loft sounds dreamy . . . high ceilings, wide-open spaces, walls of windows, and a hint of industrial style are incredible features—until you try to outfit that authentically cool space in a style you can live with. One of the key benefits to living in a loft is the open-concept layout of one-room living. But that's also a big part of the challenge. Even an open plan still needs to be able to function as a collection of distinct rooms in order to meet the needs and challenges of everyday life. While you may not have an abundance of doors and windows to divide "this" area from "that," it's still possible to create a home environment that allows you to experience and enjoy each and every inch of your loft while tailoring different areas to the various functions of everyday life.

GALLERY WALL ←

Don't be discouraged if you're on a tight budget for art. You can make your own! All of these images are close-up details of urban graffiti that were snapped on a digital camera (even a lowly point-and-shoot can work wonders). The ready-made frames are inexpensive and come complete with a mat, so all you need to do is select your favourite images, enlarge and print them at your local photo shop, and pop them into frames. You'll have a fabulous gallery wall at a price you can afford!

DETAIL OF FRAME SPACING ←

Create a grid. For best results with a gallery-style installation, allow a consistent width and height between each image. These have minimum space between so the group reads as a unified whole. When installing your own gallery wall, try laying all the pieces out on the floor to make sure you are happy with the arrangement before you swing the hammer.

WOVEN ART ↞

There's no universal rule about what can be deemed "art," so let your imagination run wild. When the budget started to run thin, I found a kilim carpet on sale for a great deal and decided to use it as a tapestry-inspired wall hanging to bring colour and pattern to the dining area. The good news is that if you ever want to use it on the floor in the future, it's still fully functional!

MASS APPEAL ↞

Create an interesting tablescape by collecting vintage, coloured glass bottles (or new ones made to look vintage). A grouping of a single type of object in a single material is a foolproof and fabulous way to accessorize. Even without flowers they look terrific as the light shines through!

TABLE WITH CONTENTS ↕

A giant table made from reclaimed wood takes centre stage in the dining area of this live/work space and does double duty as a boardroom table and gathering place for friends. With ingenious storage doors camouflaged into the columnar bases, it's easy to hide office clutter or extra supplies and make that quick change from "work" to "live" when evenings and weekends arrive.

MATERIAL MIX ↕

Taming an industrial space into something that also has warmth and texture and feels like home can be challenging. To find the right mix, I incorporated equal amounts of cool-industrial with warm-residential influences. The charcoal-grey steel dining chairs and modern Edison bulb light fixture reflect a nod to industrial elements (like the original factory windows), while the softer elements such as the table, wall hanging, and end chairs add some much-needed warmth.

CUT IT OUT ↕
Creating the illusion of distinct spaces within an open-concept whole is an effective tool for maximizing your functionality and storage. A floating wall is easy to construct with metal studs and drywall and acts as a divider between the living and dining areas, while providing the opportunity to put a bookshelf or storage piece on either side of the wall to service each area. The 5-foot-by-5-foot cutout in the wall allows the light to shine through from the bank of windows.

KEEP YOUR OPTIONS OPEN ⫯

If you're renting and worried about making long-term commitments to furniture, why not take a more flexible approach? A piece of butcher block sitting on top of standard file cabinets sprayed in a funky, vivid colour is an easy and inexpensive way to get a big work surface, and the pieces can always be repurposed separately in your next home! The suede-covered armchair is the mate to the dining room end chairs and can easily pivot between desk and dining table as needed. When entertaining, a quick tidy of the desktop will allow it to do double duty as a bar or buffet.

GO BACK IN TIME ⫯

To balance the vintage quotient with a new desk and chair, try finding vintage desktop organizers at secondhand shops. A pair of old index-card file drawers makes great desktop storage, a vintage, painted wastebasket will remind you of school days past, and a wood in-and-out file with metal accents is far more chic than what you'll find in your local office-supply store.

PATTERNED PERFECTION

The idea of finding a home and putting down roots is an alluring goal, and a commendable accomplishment. Settling in, raising a family, and building a community are milestone events. But sometimes, the longer you stay, the more you accumulate, and the less you love the space in which you live. With two teenage kids, this busy family was ready to start a new chapter at home and called on me to bring youthful energy and laid-back design to their century-old row house.

GET ARTSY ➻

There's no rule about what can be "art." It should be whatever speaks to you and makes you feel happy. Since I was borrowing some references from English style (the William Birch–style sofa, the floral motif, the bold use of colour on the sofa), I decided to go the distance and create a wall of decorative floral plates. Forget precious and pricey and poke around garage sales, flea markets, thrift stores, and consignment shops to get good deals on individual plates in varied sizes and you'll be able to create an instant, impactful, and inexpensive great wall of china!

SET THE SCENE ➻

Dining tables come in all shapes and sizes, and at all price points. If you want to score a steal, you need to be flexible on style, so it's best to shop for key pieces early in the game before you've nailed a firm design direction. On a visit to a vintage dealer filled with estate-sale furniture, I unearthed a solid, vintage French-style table complete with extension leaves for less than you'd pay for a new piece. With a small investment in refinishing costs, I was able to give my new old find the Cinderella treatment and tie the wood tones of the room together.

DARE TO DAYDREAM ➻

I've always been a big fan of the daybed. In my mind's eye, I must envision myself as a lounger, with hours to spend reclining, reading, and relaxing (although that's not my reality). Instead of pushing a daybed up against the wall, I suggest using it in place of a sofa as a room divider. Since a daybed is backless, you can perch on it from either side, lean on either end, or get cozy and horizontal, plus it keeps your sight lines open from one room to the next. Since you'll gain at least 6 inches of depth by eliminating a sofa back, the daybed can be a valuable space-saver in a small room.

BE A SAVVY SHOPPER ✎

You may have always thought that silk drapes were out of your price range, but the key to fabric success is knowing where to shop. You can always find reasonably priced dupioni silk at garment fabric stores, and it comes in hundreds of colours. Adding a 6-inch-wide accent band down the side in a patterned taffeta is an accessible indulgence since you won't need much yardage (of course, you can also save any scraps and use them for pillows).

GET A BOLD START ⬍
If you want to create a fun, vibrant mood, get off on the right foot by using an overscaled, contemporary floral pattern to set the tone. This cotton floral was very affordable, is printed on a linen textured background, and feels anything but fussy. Instead of using your chosen floral in the traditional way (on a sofa or drapes), try it on an armchair (or two). A giant print on a smallish chair creates an interesting contrast in proportion and accentuates any curvaceous lines the chair might have. In a small space, try to focus on pieces that have height, yet are compact.

MAKE AN ENTRANCE ⬍
Painting the outside of your front door an exciting colour isn't a novel idea—it's common practice! But, if your entry door leads right into the main living space, why not consider tying the colour of your door to the palette of the room? There's no rule that says both sides of the door need to be the same hue, so spread out the fan deck and pick a fun shade to add some life to your entry—and exit!

WORK A LITTLE MAGIC ←
Renovation isn't the only way to make a petite window appear larger. Instead of extending your drapes beyond the window frame by the standard 5 or 6 inches, add a little extra and trick the eye. By taking the drapes 14 inches beyond the window, you can make the window read larger than it is. Adding a band of a darker accent colour to the outside edge of the drapes also helps to draw the eye outward and anchors the sides.

HIGH-RISE CONDO

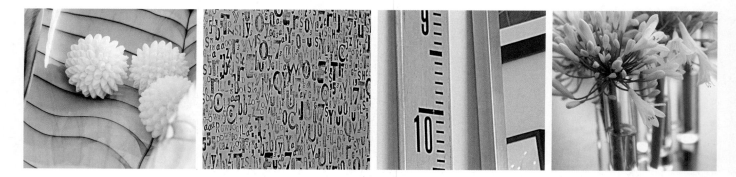

The condominium is a modern solution that offers turnkey, easy living for those who prefer a worry-free existence with great skyline views over garbage disposal, yard work, and snow removal. Amenities and conveniences aside, the big challenge I've always faced with condo living is the pervasive element of sameness. As someone who strives to be an individual, I have a tough time swallowing the cookie-cutter approach to homes. I can't fault the compelling argument for the ease factor of condo life, so I decided to try my hand at lending style and substance to a brand-new blank-canvas box in the heart of the downtown core.

CREATE FLOW ➙

Since many homeowners find that their dining table only gets occasional use for sit-down dinners, a round table offers a flexible solution. At the entrance to a large room, a round table can act as a presentation piece that makes a welcoming statement each time you walk in and also helps facilitate flow through the space instead of creating a blockade with sharp edges.

CURATE YOUR OWN EXHIBIT ➙

I was imagining floor-to-ceiling photography to build on my vision of a gallery aesthetic, but fitting a wall of gallery-priced purchases wasn't in the budget. Ever a believer in the power of a little DIY, I headed out into the neighbourhood on a glorious day with digital camera in hand, searching for inspiration and architectural interest. I'm no pro and would never undermine the true value of art, but if you've got a tight budget and are feeling creative, I say load up your digital with a memory card, learn how to master your camera's settings (most new models allow you to actually shoot in black and white instead of colour), and snap away. Thanks to inexpensive printing and ready-to-go frames, you can create a gallery installation in your own home!

JAZZ IT UP ⬍

Without trim details or architectural interest to lean on, it's tough to up the ante on the raw space in a new condo. Creating an environment that draws you in and helps you transition through the different areas can be a challenge, so I'm always looking for ways to make it a memorable experience. Installing a contemporary wallpaper pattern with metallic circles against a white background establishes a subtle yet effective transition between the kitchen and living area while leading the eye to the principal space. An area that might have been a missed opportunity became a dynamic vignette of contrast, pattern, and texture.

DARE TO BE DIFFERENT ⬍

If all of your friends and neighbours are flocking to retailers who specialize in brand-new decor solutions, why not try something different and embrace the idea of curating an interesting assortment of unique finds to create a home that transcends condo cliché? By making the decoration of your home a process akin to a scavenger hunt, you'll be rewarded with a finished product that bears no resemblance to any other unit in the building. You don't need to invest in collector-level antiques, but I do believe that you can create instant soul in a new home when you commit to pieces with a history.

MAX OUT THE SPACE ←

Since condo designs tend to focus on the importance of a single, large living space, it's best to devise a furniture layout that makes the most of every bit of available room. If you spend most of your time in one room, it should live as large as possible, allowing maximum flexibility, storage, seating, comfort, and style. Try to push your furnishings outward to the perimeter of the room so you can define the areas and make them feel spacious and open instead of cluttered. Allow the traffic to flow through your furniture arrangement instead of around it, and you'll be amazed at how much bigger it will feel.

SMOOTH IT OUT ↘

There are some undeniable detractors in condos, and stipple or stucco ceilings are a common complaint for many owners. The good news is they are relatively easy to fix. If the stucco is new or unpainted, it can usually be sprayed with water to soften it, and then be scraped off. It's not complicated, but it's labour-intensive, and it's best tackled at the start of the project, as an empty space is preferred for ease and mess control!

RUSTIC COUNTRY LODGE

When it comes to country living, I favour a lighthearted and laid-back approach defined by casually elegant materials that emphasize comfort and carefree living. On an idyllic property, where both privacy and natural beauty were abundant in equal measures, a petite century-old stone cottage was enhanced with an open-concept great-room addition to welcome grown children and grandchildren to a weekend home with easy, breezy style.

KEEP IT SPARE ←

You won't want to spend every waking moment dusting knick-knacks and picking up after guests (which you will undoubtedly have once you make the move to a country lifestyle), so avoid the clutter and streamline your space to have as few useful pieces as possible. Take a less-is-more approach and outfit your living area with the minimum number of generously scaled pieces of furniture to service your needs. Instead of cramming too many upholstered pieces into a seating grouping, go for deep and comfy sofas and chairs that encourage lounging, then tuck a couple of extra chairs into empty corners and they'll be ready to draw into the room whenever a crowd comes calling, yet you won't find yourself tripping over them daily.

BLUR THE BOUNDARIES ←

Since country life revolves around a seamless transition between indoors and out, you can relax the rules and bring exterior references indoors. A large-scale iron lantern illuminates the main living area in a spare and unadorned style while allowing the intricate rusted French iron chandelier to take centre stage in the adjacent dining area. Even in a single room you can define the areas and give them individual personality.

PANEL DISCUSSION ←

To minimize the use of drywall while adding texture and country-appropriate materials, consider applying beadboard or V-groove panelling to your vaulted ceilings. If you're planning on using a solid painted finish, save the time (and expense) of painstakingly installing the boards one at a time and use MDF-sheet wood panelling, sold in large-format sizes like drywall. To reference the cottage-style aesthetic, the panelling here is intersected with decorative beams that add another layer of texture and interest to the cathedral ceiling.

ENJOY THE SIMPLE LIFE ⇡
Instead of glitz and glam, country style works best with unadorned,
natural elements. A woven table runner adds a touch of softness to the table,
a row of chunky glass candlesticks in varying heights will add a warm glow
in the evening hours, and fresh-from-the-farm produce adds a decorative
accent that epitomizes the field-to-table lifestyle.

PLAN FOR A CROWD ⇡
Unexpected guests and cramped quarters at mealtimes are part of the joy
of family gatherings. To ensure you've always got room for one more at the table,
consider a mix-n-match approach to your seating plan. Reproduction, painted
wooden chairs offer individual seats on one side, while an antique church bench
provides a spot to squeeze in little ones (or those who like to get cozy). The misty-
grey blue on the chairs references the palette of the living room accents, and the
aged pine reinforces the honey-toned warmth of the floors and tabletop.

SNUGGLE UP ↘

In a space composed of simple textiles and unadorned finishes,
there's still plenty of room for texture and pattern. Rely on useful
accessories, such as soft and cozy throws, to layer in a bit of pretty pattern
and indulge your appetite for luxury. Diving under a woven throw while
sitting fireside after a long country walk is one of life's simple pleasures.

LET THERE BE LIGHT ↗

If you are lucky enough to spend time in the country, you'll likely want to maximize
your views to outside, so you always feel connected to the landscape. Instead of
closing off rooms with solid wood doors, consider keeping the vistas in view by
installing sliding pocket doors with glazed panels. On a brisk day they can be kept
closed while allowing the light to stream in, and they disappear when not in use.

THE
KITCHEN

I think of kitchens as gathering spaces for family. The kitchen is in high demand from sunrise through sunset, servicing every member of the family. It runs the gamut from mission control for organizing the household to an arts and crafts centre for the kids, snack station, wine bar, and computer portal. Not to mention gathering place, diner, and bistro. I've always felt that kitchens should be welcoming, not intimidating, and laid out with a natural ease and flow to deliver the functionality, design features, and efficiency you demand, yet also all of the comfort you crave and associate with home and family. My childhood kitchen was small, yet pretty objects were always on the windowsill — a vase, a lovely piece of glass, or pottery from a trip, and a glowing candle. Like a little curated gallery, the windowsill evolved over time and became an area of my mom's personal expression, even within a small space. That evolution of personal expression was so important to me then, and still is now — especially in the kitchen.

SILVER CITY CONDO

Condo kitchens aren't known for their spacious proportions or functional layouts. Instead, they tend to be diminutive and dysfunctional, lacking in both counter space and storage capabilities. In many new buildings, the kitchens are so small, they practically come with a maximum-occupancy warning that can't exceed one person. Since the party always happens in the kitchen, I love having a decent-sized space to work with. That's the advantage of buying a run-down unit in an older building. This kitchen was in the wrong place, devoid of light, and cut off from the action in the living area, but by removing partition walls, it became a sleekly styled culinary oasis.

CUSTOMIZE IT ↞

I want it all. Always have, always will. Every project has its budget limitations, and they always add up faster than you hope. If a total overhaul of your home is on the agenda, you'll need to keep your eye on the bottom line at every turn. To pull back on the budget reins, I based this kitchen on simple, in-stock slab cabinetry doors. Made of MDF, these doors already have a painted finish, so respraying them in a new smoky charcoal tone simply treats the original white finish as a base coat for a custom colour scheme at a fraction of the cost of a true custom kitchen.

REFLECT ON IT ↞

Putting a mirror in your bedroom, bathroom, or entryway may be second nature, but perhaps it never struck you as a necessity in the kitchen. Forget using it to primp and preen, and think about how useful a mirrored surface can be to visually enlarge a space or to draw in views and sight lines that you wouldn't otherwise benefit from. Installing slices of grey smoked mirror in between natural-walnut floating shelves draws your eye all the way to the back wall of the kitchen and reflects the length of the hallway, plus it allows you to see what's happening behind you while cleaning up at the sink.

STEP IT UP ↘

Knowing how you cook and what your habits are is important when laying out your kitchen. If you tend to make a mess and leave a trail of dirty pots and pans in your wake, raising the height of your breakfast bar to hide your path of destruction from view is probably a wise move. Creating a raised bar also affords the opportunity to use the narrow bar for the display of pretty objects without fear of knocking them over when you're in the throes of whipping up a feast.

BUILD THE GREAT WALL ↗

Since storage is a major concern in many condominium residences, it's important to designate as much room as possible to well-thought-out storage solutions to help you conquer the inevitable clutter and keep things tucked away in their proper place. To accommodate the need for a stacked washer/dryer in the unit, a full-height, wall-to-wall installation of pantry cupboards was chosen to house the machines in one cupboard, with dishes and dry-goods storage in the next.

Installing full-height cabinets will reduce your available counter space, but I compensated by extending the main counter run into the circulation/hall space, thereby creating additional prep space and a bar counter with seating for two.

SPOTLIGHT IT ↗

Condo ceilings are known for being challenging, as they are usually a solid concrete slab that limits your ability to redesign your lighting p an and get the beams
of light focused just where you need them. Creating a dropped ceiling will allow
you to put pot lights and pendants wherever your heart desires, but it will also
gobble up about 6 inches of ceiling height. Think about other sources of illumination that allow you to light up your workspace, such as these puck lights that
anchor the ends of the open shelves and send a beam of light along their length.

GET JAZZY ↗

In my book, saving in one area naturally begets splurging in another.
The frugality of using ready-to-install cabinetry for the cupboards led
to the creation of a groovy graphic backsplash rendered in natural stone
and installed with painstaking attention to detail. By combining rectangular
white marble "bricks" set in a herringbone pattern with single strips of confetti-
dot marble mosaic, a unique backsplash detail emerged that adds punch
and pizzazz to the kitchen and elevates it way beyond average.

FAMILY-FRIENDLY KITCHEN

Filled with shiny maple cabinets and glossy black counters, the kitchen in this home presented a major personality conflict with its new owners—one that could only be resolved through drastic measures and a demolition crew. While some homeowners are flexible and could easily live with a multitude of style directions, others have a definitive personal style that permeates everything from wardrobe to interior design in a cohesive manner. This home belonged to just such a client. After dabbling with colour, the lady of the house had conviction and confidence that only a white kitchen with black accents would do. With whimsical accessories and lighthearted touches, this all-white creation provides the backdrop for a bustling family home.

GO DINER STYLE ↠

The casual ease of a simple diner meal is appealing for a few reasons. The durable finishes, classic white dishes, and unfussed approach to churning out tasty meals seems well connected to how we live at home. Every meal isn't a production, and it's definitely not fancy. So if relaxed and friendly is more your style than polished and sophisticated, take a page from the ready-to-serve stacks of chunky white dishes in the serving line of any diner and create the same look at home by leaving the bottom section of your cabinets open. Stacking your everyday dishes in plain view means everyone will always be able to find what he or she is looking for, and the pieces you use most often will be within easy reach, whether plating up the lunch special or unloading the dishwasher.

STICK WITH A THEME ↠

After deciding on a colour theme, it's wise to follow the path and allow that direction to guide your decisions. To maintain the light and bright, cloudlike palette in this kitchen, I opted for full overlay panels on the fridge and dishwasher so they blend right into the cabinetry, white counters, white stools, white dishes, and even white knobs on the appliances. In essence, anything available in white was ordered in white. This sort of commitment to a palette definitely makes for swift decision-making as you take deliberation out of the equation.

LET IT FLOW ↕
The end of every cabinet run in your kitchen requires a finishing panel,
or a gable, to connect the counter to the floor and clad the interior-box
construction of the cabinets with material that matches the door profiles.
For a contemporary finishing touch, consider a waterfall edge on your counters
that uses a mitred corner to create a seamless flow of countertop material
that runs all the way to the floor. While this adds to the budget since it requires
fabrication of additional countertop material, it gives a supersleek finishing
detail and provides a more durable outside edge in high-traffic areas.

TUCK IT IN ⤒

Every kitchen layout is unique, but I've found that almost every renovation results in a quirky space that can be turned into a useful station of some sort. In this case, what was once a doorway got filled in by a run of cabinetry, leaving an awkward gap on the back side facing the mudroom. Adding a small drawer and extending the counter into the nook turned a nothing space into a compact work area. Since laptops and tablets are often in the midst of kitchen chaos, this provides an out-of-the-way spot to set up shop.

WRAP IT UP ↘

When placing your sink with a view to the garden, you may find that the space between counter and sill is limited, thereby posing a challenge for trim and finishing details. Standard wood trim is best kept away from sources of water, but continuing your counter material up the backsplash and across the sill is a streamlined and durable solution that's strong enough for the inevitable overspray during cleanup.

MAKE IT A FAMILY AFFAIR ←

Even the most beautiful spaces need to be filled with life and spirit to come alive, so designate an area where everyone can participate in the creative collaboration by installing a large "mission control" tackboard. This magnetic blackboard invites all members of the family to proudly share their latest creation and puts it on display for all to see.

SLEEK LOFT EATERY

Loosely defined borders are an advantage in a loft kitchen. Without being confined by walls and divided spaces, you can allot as much or as little area to the kitchen as you feel is appropriate for your lifestyle. For a young urbanite who enjoys throwing the doors wide open to entertain friends in his authentic downtown loft, the focus was on styling a sleek, contemporary kitchen able to accommodate an intimate get-together or a big bash.

REACH FOR THE TOP ←←

Any cabinetry you install in a room should be appropriately scaled to the height of the walls. While you may not have need for storage that stretches the entire vertical height of your walls, a single run of short cabinets can look out of place, so stacking your cabinets will create the best overall presentation and undoubtedly offer additional storage that you can put to good use.

DABBLE IN DIY ←←

Your backsplash doesn't have to be made of tile or stone, so think what you can achieve with a simple DIY solution. I made this backsplash by purchasing 3-foot lengths of $1/4$-inch poplar wood in varying widths. Each board was painted in latex paint colours that referenced the hues in the main room, then lightly sanded to distress the finish and treated with a couple of coats of latex urethane to give a durable, protective finish. A piece of tile trim in aluminum runs across the top and holds all of the boards in place while creating a neatly finished edge, and the boards were glued to the wall using construction adhesive. With a little bit of effort. you can create a unique and dramatic backdrop for your cabinetry, painted in any colours you desire.

PULL UP A SEAT ←←

When embracing authentic loft style, your choice of materials is key. Sleek, simple, and hard-wearing stainless steel cabinetry doors and gables add that element of loft chic, while antiqued brass cabinetry pulls introduce a vintage industrial vibe (and allow you to see exactly what's behind each door thanks to handy labels). Backless metal stools tend to be less expensive than fully upholstered barstools and continue on the theme of flexibility and industrial styling thanks to chunky wheels.

OPEN CONCEPT ↕

When you are trying to install an eye-catching kitchen on an accessible budget, inexpensive ready-made shelf supports are a handy way of installing a wide-open display shelf. Paint the unfinished wood in the shade of your choice, then create an impactful display shelf by topping the brackets with a thick piece of natural, unfinished lumber. The board should be at least an inch thick to provide adequate support and not warp.

BAKER'S DELIGHT

When your kitchen is due for an upgrade and it's time to give the heart of your home an overhaul, creating a fresh new look doesn't necessitate a bold move toward contemporary style. If classic vintage details are more your style than edgy modern lines, never fear—it's easy to create a kitchen that infuses today's modern conveniences with a few nods to nostalgic old-school charm and character.

———

COUNTRY CHARMERS ➤
Search flea markets and yard sales for charming country stools to perch in your kitchen for a nominal investment. These reproduction country pine stools were given new life with a fresh coat of robin's-egg-blue paint.

STACK IT UP ⬆

Even awkward spaces can accommodate useful storage. Install a shelf that runs across the top of the cabinets as an area to display pretty serving pieces like these pedestal cake plates. Pantry cabinets don't need to be deep to be useful. You can create a custom pantry cabinet that is divided by compartments with adjustable shelves to suit your storage needs.

PANTRY PRIDE ↘

Pantry basics and baking dry goods usually come in plastic packages that are tricky to keep organized in your cupboards. So buy a collection of inexpensive flip-top sealer jars and use them to keep your dry goods well organized, clearly labeled, and easy to find.

WHITE OUT ⬆

Have fun with your faucet — mix and match finishes to get a look you love. You don't need to settle for plain chrome or brushed-steel finishes; some faucets can be ordered in a variety of colours. A glossy white-painted faucet with chrome knobs is a fresh and bright addition to a sunny kitchen.

ADD AN ACCENT ⬍
Even little details can help reinforce your colour scheme. These chrome and wood vintage handles were painted the same colour as the stools to add a touch of fun to the all-white cabinets.

WHITE IS ALWAYS RIGHT ⬅
Make your kitchen timeless by selecting classic finishes such as white for all the big-decision items, such as cabinets, counters, and even appliances, but don't miss the opportunity to have fun with colour. It's easy to make it seem as if you used a lot of colour even if it's just limited to inexpensive and easy-to-change accessories such as countertop accessories, ceramics, and dishes.

POWDERY CONFECTION

When I design a kitchen, my number-one criterion is to achieve a functional layout with long runs of counter space for prep areas. I don't strictly abide by the layout rule which puts stove, sink, and refrigerator in a triangle close to one another, as I find it often creates cramped corners of usable space and leaves the chef feeling crowded and chopping in the dark. Even in a relatively small space I try to focus on making the chef feel that there's room to spread out.

SHADES OF LIGHT ↦
Bold, dramatic, cutting-edge colours are fun to experiment with and create stunning results for adventurous homeowners, but my goal of designing spaces with enduring style and timeless choices guides me to suggest that clients choose a lighter shade of pale for the fixed elements, such as cabinets, and then let loose with a bold accent paint colour on the walls that is both inexpensive and easy to change if your taste changes

TWO IS BETTER THAN ONE ↦
My suggestion for a light cabinetry colour doesn't mean it has to be white. Torn between the desire for something new and my desire for longevity, I settled on light, but not white, with pale grey for the gables, the crown, and the open shelves, and a light cream for only the door and drawer fronts. The grey and cream pick up the variations in both the counters and the backsplash and create a subtle two-tone effect. I can't say it's bold, but it's better than plain old vanilla!

BE TRANSPARENT ↕
In addition to open shelving, I often also install textured glass cabinets—they add a bit of sparkle, yet disguise the contents due to the patterned surface. By installing wide "reeded" glass horizontally instead of in the standard vertical orientation, you can create a more contemporary effect while introducing a hint of texture.

PUSH THE LIMIT ↦
The standard rules suggest leaving clearances of 42 to 48 inches to open a refrigerator, dishwasher, or oven or to circulate around a counter, but I tend to push the limits and leave a little less (usually not more than 36 inches) in favour of achieving more counter and storage space. Let's face it, preparing meals is not a group effort in most homes, and there need not be enough space to choreograph a dance routine. In all my years of pinching clearances, no clients have ever complained after their kitchen renovation.

OPEN UP ↘

Every kitchen I design has to have a balance of practical storage and pretty display space. I'm a collector of decorative ceramics and glass, so I always like to have some of my treasures on display in my kitchen. Open shelves are best when used to display a single collection of a single colour, but clear glass isn't very impactful and shows the dust, so stick to sculptural yet practical pieces that are used regularly. This way the shelves become a functional area for the everyday items you need close at hand.

HARDWARE MATTERS ↕

There are two components to this thought. First, don't cheap out on your hardware—it's the final embellishment of your kitchen, so make sure to choose something you love. Second, think about whether you really want handles or whether knobs will do. Handles are often available in more trendy profiles, but the disadvantage is that you need to drill two holes to install a handle and only one for a knob. If your tastes change, you can always switch out a knob for a different style, but it's not so easy with a handle to find an alternative with the same spacing for the screws. Something to keep in mind if resale is on the horizon . . .

OPTIMIZE YOUR OPTIONS ↕

An island is a common item on renovating wish lists, but I find a peninsula is often far more effective, especially when space is an issue. If you are thinking about removing all or part of the wall between the kitchen and the dining room, a peninsula may be your best option. It allows you to create a clearer delineation between a more polished dining area and the functional needs of the kitchen space, plus it offers great storage opportunities by allowing you to install back-to-back cabinetry servicing both rooms.

RAISED BAR COUNTER ↕

A bar counter with an overhang performs two functions: the raised bar section allows pull-up bar seats in an area that would be too cramped with an island, and, of course, the elevated counter also helps hide the chef's unsightly messes.

CHERRY POP KITCHEN

When renovating a house that's over a hundred years old, the style debate revolves around how to revitalize it. Do you strip it back to the structure and finish it with a cool modern mandate, or do you restore the past while updating it with historical architectural details and accents? For this homeowner, the fine balance was achieved through an extensive renovation that embraced traditional ornamentation and an interior that marries the best of both worlds.

——————

GET READY TO GO ↦

The key to managing a tight budget is being practical and pragmatic about what you can and cannot afford. Forget about a custom kitchen and head to your local big-box store or home outfitter for solutions that are fashion forward and wallet friendly. Keep in mind that buying a ready-to-go kitchen doesn't mean you can't customize it to make it your own. There are oodles of door profiles, sizes, and configurations that can be manipulated to stunning effect. The amount you'll save by using stock elements will enable some flexibility on other aspects of your kitchen reno. An off-the-rack solution isn't suited to every project, but if you're trying to keep an eye on the overall investment in your home, it can be a winning solution.

PLAY IT SAFE ↦

Suggesting a white kitchen isn't exactly groundbreaking design advice, but I can tell you from experience that it's hard to go wrong with white and much easier to err in colour. When it's dressed up properly, it can be tough to tell the difference between an inexpensive versus an expensive white kitchen, but the same cannot be said for a red one, so I'd recommend playing it safe. There's plenty of room to make your mark when it comes to accents and accessories (and you are far less likely to wake up regretting your choice of a bold red vase than an all-red kitchen).

DON'T BE TOO SERIOUS ‡

Inject some lighthearted fun into your all-white kitchen with a happy colour that reflects the energy of your personality. A few high-impact, low-investment hits of colour can satiate your desire to make a bold statement. I upholstered a steel bench and counter stools in wipeable and indestructible cherry red vinyl, while the table settings and kitchen accoutrements continue the red theme and introduce graphic patterns and whimsical energy, all on an inexpensive budget. If the desire for blue, green, yellow, or orange should strike anytime soon, it's a quick fix to replace the red!

DETAILS ‡

The all-important key to success with creating what I call the "off-the-rack bespoke" approach is to not make it a one-stop shopping adventure. It's tempting to just get it all done at once, but sourcing a few elements from other retailers will give your kitchen a signature look. Designer hardware, lighting, and accessories will dress up your kitchen and help you achieve that high-end look. The fashion gurus will tell you that it's okay to have some basics from mass-market retailers as long as you have a hint of "label" that makes a statement. A classic George Nelson "bubble" lamp over the dining table, hand-screened fabric from a local designer, Italian cabinetry hardware, and a sleek sink and faucet were the little indulgences that elevated the overall look of the kitchen to a higher level. Amidst a sea of white, these are the elements that catch the eye and make the right design statement.

EYE-LEVEL IMPACT ↕

Tackling "high/low" successfully means knowing where to cut back and where to invest. Concrete, hardwood, or stone floors would be nice to have, but none of those options were in our budget, so I focused attention on what is seen at eye level, and let the floors be a neutral backdrop. I'd prefer to have a marble mosaic backsplash and custom-fabricated quartz counters over a pricey floor. The linoleum floor has the palette and pattern of concrete, but cost a fraction of the price — and it was done in a day, which is not only budget-friendly but helps with the ever-stressful time line of any renovation.

CABINETRY CONFIGURATION ↕

To get the best overall look from your installation, try to create interesting configurations with your cabinetry and keep the layout symmetrical. If you look at European kitchen design practices, you'll notice a uniformity and repetition to the layout (they tend to favour lower units created entirely of wide "pot and pan"-style drawers, full-height pantries with ample storage, and horizontally mounted cabinets, often executed in a contrasting material. Instead of chopping up the layout with all sorts of tiny door/drawer combinations and finicky small cabinets, it's best to opt for large banks of doors and drawers that give a harmonious visual impression.

RETRO LUNCH COUNTER

Not every kitchen overhaul requires a Dumpster and a full back-to-the-studs gut job. If you've got a space with "good bones" and quality craftsmanship, it may be easier and less expensive to keep what works and redress what you've got instead of buying all new. If your existing cabinets are still functioning properly and are made of solid wood with a door profile that you feel you can work with, I say keep them and focus on making them look sparkling and new!

GO BEYOND THE BROWN ↤

Your cabinets may be an unappealing shade of brown right now, but you need to get past the current state and focus on what they might become with a stroke of a brush. A single homogenous shade can be reworked into a multitoned palette that enables you to breathe new life into a drab old shell. Be a bit daring and infuse a light, bright hue to complement the creamy-white cabinetry. An island is a relatively small area, isn't a huge investment to paint, and can easily be changed to a safer shade if the urge ever strikes.

GET A HANDLE ↤

One of the biggest detractors in a "days gone by" kitchen is the hardware. If you've got face-mounted hinges (as opposed to the hidden variety that are commonly used now) and want to swap them out, you just need to take a sample of the existing hinge and match the size in a new finish and style. Replacing your cabinetry

knobs and handles is an effective way to create an inexpensive update — just make sure you choose the new fittings before you spray the doors in a fresh finish so you know whether the screw holes from the old hardware need to be patched and covered. There are many different offsets in cabinetry handles, and it's not always easy to find a match.

SAVE & SPLURGE ↤

According to my math, what you save in one area should be available for reallocation where it makes the most impactful design statement, so I splurged on new counters for full gourmet effect. Quartz-composite counters come in many colours and combinations. With a flecked design that combined all our chosen colours (including a glint of metal) and a look vaguely reminiscent of terrazzo floors, I felt this material had just the right amount of retro to bridge the old and new influences.

PLAY WITH PATCHWORK
When you're looking to make changes in an existing space, knowing your limits is key. Replacing the floor while keeping the cabinets means you need to install your new floor choice in and around the existing cabinets. Changing to a stone-tile floor would raise the overall height of the tiled areas and reduce the baseboards, not to mention that it also costs about twice the price of other options. Since I was hankering for a retro diner vibe, I chose to install linoleum floor tiles. With a marbled, easy-care finish and more than a dozen fun colours to choose from, I opted for a trio of spring-fresh flooring tiles that look as pretty as a patchwork quilt!

BE AUTHENTIC
If you want your newly redecorated kitchen to have realistic retro roots, you need to add some authentic elements to the mix. Vintage machine-age stools provide an authentic perch at the newly created island bar. And building on the theme of cool metal accents, large pendant lights and a chrome dining table infuse the ethereal palette with sleek style and add polish to a simple kitchen overhaul.

HAVE A SEAT ↤

Since many families use their kitchen for the majority of casual meals, having a dining area that's both practical and pretty is an important priority. Vintage bamboo brings a light touch to the sunny dining area, and the chairs are family friendly since only the seats are upholstered. Any residue from sticky fingers can be wiped off the backs, while the seats are covered in an easy-to-scrub cotton pattern.

STEP IT UP ↕

To fill a void in a window to an adjoining room, I discovered that stair treads provide an easy answer to floating shelves. More than an inch thick, 12 inches deep, 48 inches long, and at less than $20 each, these ready-to-go treads from the building-materials aisle of a big-box store make great open display shelves that lend custom cachet to an off-the-shelf solution. When you are repainting the entire kitchen, it's easy to tweak a few storage details, then unify them with the magic of paint.

SWAP IT OUT ↤

Turn a favourite mirror frame into a household organizational tool by having the mirror replaced with a fabric-covered piece of bulletin board. Located right beside the kitchen door, this handy backboard helps keep everyone in the loop on the week's events.

SUNNY SERVERY

When you're house hunting, myriad factors influence your buying decision. Neighbourhood, curb appeal, size, value, and character are among the chart-topping elements that inform our choice of home. And when the nesting instinct kicks in, we can quickly convince ourselves to see past a laundry list of flaws that need to be addressed. But eventually, the detractors need to be dealt with, and that was the case with this kitchen. Tucked away at the back of the house, with an unworkable layout (and unbearable brown and yellow vintage finishes), an immediate solution was needed to turn it from a '60s flashback into a modern-day family-friendly hub.

LET THE LIGHT IN ←

Gaining a bar area and room for counter stools is a major advantage to removing a section of wall and connecting your kitchen to the adjacent room, but another invaluable advantage is the amount of light that floods into your kitchen by opening up your sight lines. Located at the back of the house, this kitchen felt dim and blocked off from the rest, but now it has sight lines all the way through the dining and living rooms, with views of the sun streaming in through the west-facing living room windows. In a house with small children, being able to see into every room makes multitasking and meal prep much easier!

HEAD TO THE COAST ←

Regardless of the fact that I live in an urban location far from the ocean, I still love a coastal look and feel that the essence of the beach-house aesthetic can be embraced and achieved anywhere, regardless of geography. Seashells, sailboats, and all things beach "themed" are a bit of a miss if you aren't actually on the water, but there's no reason to take a pass on the easy, breezy ambiance created by a watery colour palette and creamy-painted furniture. In addition to delivering a lighthearted look, painting your table and chairs is a surefire way to unify elements from different sources in different wood tones, as it looks perfectly coordinated once it's coated in glossy white paint.

BE TRANSPARENT ⭡

If the goal of opening spaces up is to create better sight lines and a brighter ambiance, you'll want to think carefully about the lighting you install. so it doesn't impede your views. To add a contemporary flavour to an Arts-and-Crafts-style home, I chose crystal-clear blown-glass shades resembling inverted brandy snifters for their sparkly finish and lighter-than-air look.

BUCK THE TRENDS ⭡

Balance efficiency and functionality with beauty and softness. Fixed elements, such as cabinetry, appliances, and flooring, will instil the the kitchen with functionality, but it's "the wrapping" that brings the space to life. I always look at the practical side of a room: you want to create a beautiful space that's relevant by today's design standards, but you don't want to be cavalier when it comes to spending renovation dollars by installing a kitchen that is driven by trend-based decisions you may soon live to regret. Always thinking of longevity, I make safe choices by opting for fixed elements in neutral tones, then I allow the story of the kitchen, its essence and personality, to happen through the lighting, paint, fabrics, and accessories.

TAKEOUT OR DINE IN? ⦚
An eat-in kitchen is a top priority for many of us, but also an unattainable goal in many older, smaller homes without a massive renovation or addition. Before you start editing your wish list and resign yourself to making do without a breakfast bar, think about whether you can reach your goal another way. By removing only the upper portion of the wall connecting the kitchen and the dining room, you can create the eat-in kitchen you've always wanted, even if you are short on space. Maintaining the lower section allows you to maximize cabinetry and counter runs on the kitchen side, while also creating the perfect foundation for a raised bar counter and a pair of stools.

MORE IS MORE ⦚
When it comes to picking paint colours, I always advocate integrating as many colours as possible into a scheme to create a dynamic palette. Even though you've created a connection by opening up the kitchen and the dining room, there's nothing that dictates using the same paint colour for all the walls. On the contrary, I think it would be a missed opportunity to go for uniform colour. To keep the kitchen light and bright, a wispy green was used to reinforce the tones in the floor, the stripes in the blinds, and the apple-green accents in the counter. In the dining room, the walls were painted an ocean-blue hue drawn from the kitchen backsplash. Each room stands alone, yet the coordinated palettes link the spaces.

MODERN COUNTRY MIX

When you hear the word *country* used in design, do you instantly envision cutesy doilies, lace, and knickknacks? If so, it's time to get acquainted with the more contemporary relative of the old-school country classics. Modern country takes the best of plein air style and marries it with a more streamlined and edgy industrial aesthetic to create a result that is thoroughly and completely in touch with contemporary lifestyles.

BE WHIMSICAL ↤
Finishing decor touches will help enhance your modern country look with winning results. The drapes are made from by-the-yard fabric printed with the pattern of an overscaled "wishie" (you know . . . the dandelion remnant that you blew on as a kid) — what's more country appropriate than that? Nothing in my book!

BLUR THE BOUNDARIES ↤
I am drawn to repetition as a means of creating harmony, such as the theme of mixing rough exterior elements with finer interior ones. The combination of rough reclaimed barn boards, vintage coach lanterns, and patio chairs reupholstered in snazzy charcoal pinstripe twill underscore the idea of mixing indoors with outdoors to create a distinct expression of country style with spirit and texture.

PANTRY PRIDE ⬍

Standard cabinetry dictates 24-inch depths for all lower cabinets, but sometimes you need to play with proportions to get everything you want out of your dream kitchen. If you're stuck with a narrower-than-desired layout and yearn for an island, installing a full wall of cabinets that is composed entirely of "uppers" with a depth of just 12 inches may help you achieve all the goals on your wish list. You can mix, match, and stack to create a wall that holds just about anything you could ever need to store.

GET ON TRACK ⬍

I can't say it often or emphatically enough, but making the commitment to seek out unique and unusual lighting is always rewarded with a better- than-average result. An overscaled vintage light fixture made of tubular piping is a fresh approach to illuminating the island with a one-of-a-kind statement.

USE YOUR LEFTOVERS ↘

It's always satisfying to turn leftovers in the kitchen into a new creation, and building materials are no exception. Instead of settling for a basic painted wall, I treated the open area above the shallow counter to the same silvery-grey barn board so it can be appreciated at eye level.

REPETITION MAKES RIGHT ⟻

Once you've embraced a graphic pattern such as her-ringbone, try repeating it in another material to reinforce the impact. Simple and inex-pensive ceramic subway tile looks snazzy when installed in the same herringbone detail as the island cladding. Pale grey grout accentuates the pattern while referencing the grey accents used throughout the room. Since this tile is one of the cheapest options on the market, you can afford to spend a bit more on the install and take it up to the ceiling for a dramatic, full-wall effect.

OLD BECOMES NEW ↕

When the goal is to take an iconic reference and reinterpret it, the trick is
to think about how you can take an element out of its "normal" context and
rework it to breathe new life into its use. When installed in a herringbone pattern
to create the wrapper for the island that anchors the kitchen, these old barn
boards become the single most interesting and effective material element in
the entire room. And don't worry—if you're not keen on hunting down old
boards out of piles in a field, you can purchase kiln-dried, reclaimed boards
from a salvage facility! When working with barn board, it's best to set the
boards within a frame to make them easy to work with and prevent them
from splintering. You can use new, smooth wood for the frame and stain
it charcoal grey to blend with the tones of the weathered boards.

BE UNIQUE ↕

There's just nothing more quintessentially country than the image of a giant, old, weathered barn, but as the farming industry changes, these majestic structures are often left to tumble down, leaving an ample supply of beautifully weathered boards that can bring texture and a smoky-grey palette to your next project. Think about how you can reinterpret unwanted materials to create dramatic results that are uniquely different.

COMPACT CITY CONDO

While you'll never have room to spare, it is certainly possible to cram more than you might imagine into a small space. And condo living in compact quarters will certainly test your resolve in achieving culinary perfection amidst confined borders. The advantage of small-space work areas is the necessity to streamline your kitchen to include only the elements you love most (so prepare to edit and purge to get the best results). Rethinking this compact condo allowed me to add additional storage and better prep space without enlarging the area an inch, all the while delivering on the demand for a grown-up glam home with polish and panache.

GET INSTANT PATINA ➻

Aside from my lifelong love of treasure hunting, I find myself drawn to vintage housewares as a way to bring old-world charm and character to brand-new blank-slate spaces. Since the objective was to lend a hint of feminine elegance to this tiny spot, I accessorized with functional, everyday items that came with a timeworn patina. Finding newly manufactured items of equivalent quality would cost far more and look too new, while these well-loved treasures echo the soft sheen on the silver-leafed fillet that accents the cabinetry.

INTERNAL REFLECTION ➻

Apartments and condominiums are generally limited to fenestration (aka windows) on a single elevation, which can leave you staring at the walls on the other three sides. If you're hankering to put a window where none exists and improve your outlook, consider where you might be able to apply mirror for maximum impact. I replaced a pair of upper cabinets with open shelves so my client could display a pretty collection of vintage glam dinnerware and serving pieces, and the antiqued mirror backdrop tricks the eye into thinking there's another room beyond (well, there actually is . . . but it's the common hallway, so this is much more elegant).

ADD METALLIC TO THE MIX

If you're living in a studio apartment, I figure your kitchen might as well be a thing of beauty. Instead of settling for standard cabinetry door profiles, you can customize a classically simple recessed Shaker panel door by adding your own signature touch with a picture-framing fillet in the finish of your choice. Generally intended to slide behind the main picture-frame profile, a fillet adds a delicate accent to a piece of art and can also uplift your cabinet doors. Since the profile is so narrow, even silver-leafed options don't cost a mint, but they add a special touch that makes your kitchen as pretty as a picture.

PLAN FOR EASY ACCESS

When space is at a premium, storage solutions should be adaptable and easy to access. Consider the convenience of a cabinet that can be loaded and unloaded from either side to make it easier to facilitate entertaining guests in a compact space. When there's only room for one person at a time in the kitchen area, a double-sided approach allows helping hands to be useful, and not underfoot. By continuing the base of the cabinet right down to the counter, this narrow tower also helps create definition between the living and kitchen areas. With the cabinet resting on a plinth made from the counter material, there's no worry about moisture from the sink damaging the lower portion of the cabinet.

ROOFTOP AERIE

Most kitchen renovations involve maxing out both cabinetry and countertop space to optimize prep and cooking functions in smaller spaces. But not every kitchen needs to follow this approach. Personal style, as well as an understanding of the habits and usage of your lifestyle, can lead to alternative design ideas. To get the best daily use out of their home, my clients decommissioned a formal dining room to reinvent it as a family room, thereby pushing everyday dining into the kitchen space. The new kitchen needed to be both conducive to prepping family meals and elegant enough to entertain in.

FIND AN ISLAND ALTERNATIVE

If you are officially moving the party into the kitchen and using your kitchen table for all your everyday meals, it's important to think about the best, most flexible solution. When not being set for mealtime, your kitchen table can double as a prep space, so choosing a style and finish to allow both functions is wise. Instead of delicate veneer surfaces, opt for a solid-wood tabletop that is neither precious nor formal. This antique, oval French wine-tasting table allows room for 8 people and, after surviving well over a hundred years of being used for food and drink, is a durable choice. If you choose a vintage or antique table with wear, scratches, and patina as part of the package, you'll be less concerned about pressing it into service at home.

TAKE TO THE SKY

White kitchens are timeless and classic and will likely never go out of style. A light kitchen is also appealing to many homeowners, as it seems bright and clean and fresh. But keeping it light can also be achieved with a hint of your favourite hue. To make this kitchen seem less sterile and more inviting, the cabinets were painted in a barely there shade of blue. One of the most stunning features of this unique kitchen is the vaulted six-siced skylight that makes it seem as though you are cooking in the clouds, so it seemed only appropriate to dress the room in tones as light and airy as a cloud.

SHOW OFF YOUR WARES

In addition to being more dynamic than plain old white, the light blue tone of the cabinetry accentuates the curated collection of creamware and transferware dishes on the open shelves, which were installed to allude to the profile of a breakfront cabinet that you would often find in a dining room, filled with china, silver, and serving pieces. Instead of being stuck behind glass and rarely used, the pieces in this open storage area are intended for everyday service.

GET A MARBLED MARBLE

No two white marble blocks are ever exactly the same. In fact, white marble can vary widely from being pure white to having a heavily veined pattern running throughout. Many would regard a light marble tile as an impractical choice for a kitchen for fear of needing to constantly clean it, but since this version of Calacatta marble is equal parts white and veined, it feels light, yet is still dark enough to stand up to wear and tear without constant maintenance.

BESPOKE SUBURBAN

Be it a new build or a renovation in an old home, the common theme in kitchen-space planning and design is to knock out walls in the quest for the ultimate open-plan "everything" space that creates a seamless transition between kitchen and family room areas (and often stretches the entire width of the house). When faced with the challenge of bringing urban designer chic to a suburban subdivision home, the mandate was to work within the confines of builder guidelines while making it appear that it was a completely custom creation.

KNOW YOUR NEEDS ←

If you expect one room to be all things to all the people in your household, you'll want to invest a little extra time planning how to make the hub of the house reflect your sense of style (and your approach to living and entertaining). Before you tackle the layout of your kitchen, prep a file that outlines your must-haves, your needs, your wish list, and any style guidelines that might help facilitate decision making. Having a good understanding of goals (both financial and stylistic) before starting the job will help you make easier and faster decisions along the way.

FAVOUR A COOLER SHADE ←

Sure, white is known for being timelessly classic, bright, and cheery, but it can also read as slightly stark and clinical. If you find you spend mostly evening hours in your kitchen and want it to have a richer, more lounge-y feel, consider dressing your cabinets in a cool charcoal tone. With two distinctly smoky shades of grey, the vibe of this kitchen easily adapts from lunch counter to wine bar depending on the hour of day.

SIZE MATTERS ←

Proportion and scale is an important element in design, but not one that is easy to define or teach, so it's generally reduced to a matter of personal taste based on whether things look "right" together. When you've got an island that's over 10 feet in length, you'll need to amp up the scale of your lighting fixtures so they become a balanced component of the overall visual statement. A pair of large lanterns with a patinated grey finish reinforces the cool tones in this kitchen while illuminating the island work surface.

PLAY THE ODDS ←

The number of fixtures you choose to install above your island is up to you, based on the amount of light you want and the number and wattage of bulbs in each fixture. If you like vintage fixtures as much as I do, just remember that your odds of finding matching fixtures decrease with every additional one you seek. You might find a pair, but what are the chances of finding a set of 3 or 4? It can even be tricky to find multiple new fixtures in stock, so it might be wise to find your fixtures before you confirm quantities with your electrician.

DISGUISE YOUR FLAWS ←

If your home doesn't have all the architectural detail you desire, just embellish. Mouldings and trim details are the hallmarks of a custom builder, yet can easily be added to any home to give it a more stately presence.

EMBELLISH YOUR ASSETS ←

Subdivision homes are famous for skimping on architectural details, and windows are no exception. When the windows in this kitchen seemed a bit too short for my liking, I decided to trick the eye by having the Roman blinds made taller than the actual windows. When mounted just below the crown moulding, the blinds enhance the height of the windows.

PLAN TO BE PRACTICAL

There's no need to avoid using fabric in your kitchen for fear of stains and spills. Simple wooden chairs can be far more welcoming when dressed with lofty seat and back cushions that make the kitchen table an inviting place to enjoy a leisurely lunch, a casual dinner, or to spread out with the weekend paper. As long as you prewash your fabrics to avoid shrinkage and make the covers removable with zipper closures, the residue of sticky fingers and messy eaters can be erased with a quick spin cycle.

CHANNEL YOUR INNER CHEF ‡

The reality is that kitchen renovations aren't cheap, but you'll reap the
rewards of doing it right both financially and experientially. Your kitchen
reno will give you the most upside for your investment dollar, as it will boost
the value of your home, and you'll hopefully derive unlimited pleasure
from all the wonderful meals you'll create on your new range. When
selecting appliances, buy the best quality you can afford, and you may
soon find that your favourite restaurant doesn't require a reservation.

GET IN THE ZONE ‡

Instead of opting for one or two heights on your island, why not have three?
A raised bar with stools separates the chaos of the prep area from the
view of the dining area and lounge, a large run of standard-height counter
for the main island offers ample room for multiple chefs working together,
while a low, table-height area provides the opportunity to create another
distinct area when entertaining, perhaps for a bar or buffet.

VICTORIAN REVIVAL

Like people, some kitchens have bold personalities that make a striking first impression. A black-and-white kitchen is bold in its high-contrast mix, but it's also a safe choice thanks to its timeless appeal. New cabinetry, reclaimed architectural elements, and plenty of room to entertain are the magic blend in a Victorian-era home that celebrates new traditional style.

THE POWER OF TWO ➳

A dark-stained island is a popular kitchen feature, but your use of accent colour doesn't need to be limited to one piece. Emphasize a two-colour scheme by selecting one finish for all lower cabinets and another for all uppers. Black is well suited to the lower cabinets, as it grounds the kitchen (and helps hide wear and tear), whereas the white uppers keep the kitchen feeling light and bright.

BLACK AND WHITE AND COLOUR ALL OVER ➳

A black-and-white kitchen will never go out of fashion and infuses your home with classic style. If you are hankering for a jolt of colour, choose a high-impact shade for the walls (repainting is an easy solution if your appetite for colour wanes). Boldly patterned black-and-cream drapes in a grapevine motif further echo the room's palette while creating a dramatic focal point at the far end of the sight line.

FABULOUS FOCAL POINT ➳

Make your island a showstopping centerpiece by adding architectural salvage that gives standard cabinetry elements a lift. I found a large pair of salvaged 3-panel doors, which I used to clad the island. One door covered the ends, and the other one ran the length of the island. To give additional support to the overhang of the counter, and to give it a bit more decorative impact, I installed a pair of antique exterior corbels, then trimmed the island with baseboard and painted everything black to unify it with the cabinetry.

DETAILS, DETAILS ←

Reinforce the unique architectural details of your design scheme by installing vintage lighting fixtures. These milk-glass pendants have clear, faceted glass bottoms, which create sparkly beams of light on the prep surface below and are visible from the entry to the house. Black details on the glass and fittings echo the colour palette of the kitchen.

DIAL UP THE DETAILS ←

Create a ticking-stripe effect on your backsplash by combining three materials to make a custom statement. Carrara marble in 4-by-18-inch strips makes up the background, while 5/8-inch bands of Nero Marquina flank a single stripe of basket-weave Thassos mosaic. If you're creating a custom pattern, be sure to spend some time laying it out before installing so you can guarantee the stripes fall in the best places.

BACKSPLASH ←

Your backsplash is a great place to mix and match materials to create a high-impact connection between the upper and lower cabinets. Since you don't need a lot of tile to cover the backsplash, it's often the best spot to splurge on decorative tile that will deliver dramatic results.

FAUCET ←

It's not all shiny metals in the world of faucets these days. A painted finish can give a traditional faucet design a modern edge when it's dressed in glossy white.

SLIDE ON IN ↕
We'd all love to cook on a professional range, but not every
budget can accommodate top-tier appliances. If you select a slide-in
range over a standard range (with a raised back), you'll get
a sleek, professional look without breaking the bank.

PULL UP A CHAIR ↕
Additional space in a kitchen is usually dedicated to a casual kitchen table,
but if you have an adjacent dining area, you might prefer to dedicate
the space to a seating/lounge area instead of duplicating the dining function
(especially if you have stools at the island, which are likely to be the best
seats in the house for gathering with friends and enjoying quick bites).

WASTE NOTHING ⫶
Once you've placed all the key elements in your kitchen into a design layout, you will likely find that you've got an awkward amount of space left over that isn't wide enough to accommodate another cupboard. Instead of adding a filler panel, you can create a slice of open shelving to store decorative pieces and cookbooks so they are always close at hand.

GET COMFY ⫶
Carry the same colour palette into the lounge area and continue to reinforce the black-and-white mix. Inexpensive yet comfortable black rattan chairs lend an indoor-outdoor vibe to the seating area, and the open construction keeps the area feeling uncluttered. A love seat covered in grey flannel provides a great spot to curl up and get comfy with your morning coffee or the weekend paper. And a coffee table with a lower shelf provides a handy spot to keep cookbooks for quick reference when dreaming up what to serve for your next dinner party.

EAT-IN OASIS

I like to think of every kitchen as a puzzle of sorts. This compact kitchen had an unworkable, flawed layout that required a total rethink. To arrive at the best layout that combines flow, function, and fashion (without throwing in the towel on fiscal responsibility), I envisioned all the components of the kitchen as individual pieces and thought about how they should work together. By creating a layout that used as much wall space as possible to provide ample storage, a sleek and streamlined kitchen was created.

SAVE SOME GREEN ←

A blank-slate white kitchen was the right starting point for many reasons, especially the budget, but I firmly believe that your budget should never limit your creativity or your desire to be different. The green-and-grey counters had so many interesting shades that I was drawn to embrace and repeat them. By spraying a few door fronts in a rich shade of bottle green, the cabinetry transcended its out-of-the-box origins and resulted in a completely custom look. You'll need to buy lacquer and pay for spraying, but that's a small investment for being able to dream in colours beyond what's available off the shelf!

ADD SOME PUNCH ←

It's always the quirky accents and the finishing touches that elevate any room from average to interesting, so why not add some impact to your lighting by rewiring vintage fixtures? A pair of green enamelled pendants practically look "dyed to match" the accents of the kitchen and provide a refreshing contrast to the more contemporary elements.

GO BACK IN TIME ←

A classic pair of galvanized stools gives an industrial edge to the design direction, while the flared profile of the legs makes them a sturdy choice for a house with little kids, as they won't tip over, and a carrying cutout in the seat makes them easy to move around. The original versions of this line date back to the '30s, which proves they're enduring from both a design and a wear perspective.

GIVE IT THE SLIP ↕

When you've got a lounge area/family room adjoining your kitchen, think practically when selecting your seating. If you've got kids and envision a laissez-faire attitude (where food may frequently migrate to the sofa), you need to make wise choices. You'll never go wrong with the flexibility and ease of slipcovers. Instead of stressing the next time someone toddles toward the chair with a marker in hand, relax, remove the slipcover, and wash it!

SET YOUR SIGHTS ON STRIPES ↢

Most mosaic tiles are sold in 12-by-12-inch sheets on a mesh backing, which makes it easy to add a contrast band. Punctuating the pale green tiles with a single line of silver creates a wide-stripe effect that reinforces the green and grey palette of the room and lends another custom element to a cost-conscious kitchen. Be sure to measure out your pattern before installing it to achieve even repetition.

MAKE IT WORK ↕

Small-scale kitchens require creative planning and constant tidying to conquer the invasion of clutter. Installing a small workstation near the kitchen that can be used for many functions is easy to accomplish with the same cabinetry. The upper cabinet contains a bar for entertaining, while the lower section is dedicated to toys and playthings within easy reach of a toddler, and the open desk with drawers is adaptable for paying bills, working on a laptop, or doing craft projects.

CREATIVE COUNTERS ↢

Cool stainless, sleek stone, and warm wood are the most common choices for counters, but not the only options, so don't forget about good old laminate. There's a veritable rainbow of hues and designs available to add style and pattern to your counters. If you consider your options, you might just find a shade that suits your style. This modern grey-and-green pattern became the jumping-off point for the colour concept of the whole space, and I never expected to design a kitchen around laminate counters!

HAVE A GOAL ↤

If there's one element you can't live without, try to work your planning around
that feature. I felt that a peninsula was a "must have" for the additional counter
space and storage it would provide. By homing in on the best location for the
peninsula, I was able to mould the layout of the rest of the kitchen around it.
The key to success is practicality, so be sure you embrace the reality of the
available space you have and try to maximize what you've got, not what you
wish you had — the road to reno success is paved with a healthy sprinkling
of reality to keep your aspirations in line with your bank account.

WRAP IT UP ↕

Your kitchen is meant to be a creative culinary space and a family gathering
place, so don't hesitate to lighten it up with touches that liven up your home.
A wide ribbon of green paint stretches over the walls and ceiling to introduce
a bit of accent green to the lounge area, while a fun DIY clock project (made
from a simple clock kit and some vinyl adhesive lettering) makes a graphic
statement on the wall as an alternative to artwork. The lesson here is simple:
think of what you can do to add unique flair and fun to your home!

BESPOKE BEAUTY

It takes all kinds of people to make the world go round, and all styles of design to suit each unique individual's aesthetic taste and functional needs. There are many universal considerations in kitchen design, such as cooking, food storage, prep space, and cleaning functions, but that is where the similarities end—let your imagination take over to create an environment that is unlike anyone else's. In a new-build home, I had the opportunity to design a bespoke kitchen that celebrates the finest materials and craftsmanship, with expert attention to detail.

HEAD FOR THE WOODS ←←

A kitchen with a natural-wood finish exudes a rich warmth due to the organic-patterned beauty of the grain. But why settle for plain old vanilla varieties such as maple and beech when there are so many beautiful species waiting to be discovered? To make the recessed panels on the cabinet fronts as exceptional as a piece of fine furniture, crotch mahogany panels were inset amidst a darker mahogany framework. The feathery woodgrain pattern occurs naturally in wood that comes from the crotch of the tree, where the branch connects to the trunk.

BE BRASSY ←←

Choosing hardware for your new kitchen is an important consideration. Like jewellery that completes an outfit, the knobs, pulls, and hinges you use in the kitchen are the finishing touches that pull the look together. For a room that takes its cues from the details and construction of fine furniture, warm brass hardware accents were selected. If you are having a hard time narrowing down your choice of knob finish, you might want to browse for other elements with a metal accent, such as lighting, passage door hardware, and even drapery hardware, to fully realize your vision in a consistent finish for all metal components.

CARVE OUT SOME PERSONAL SPACE ↕

In a roomy kitchen, you'll have the luxury of long runs of counter space to spread out on when making gourmet feasts. Before you commit to keeping all of your countertops at a uniform height, review the plans and consider whether you have sufficient counter runs to accommodate a small desk area at standard table height. A compact desk area can be a handy spot to review recipes for meal planning, keep up with correspondence and daily mail, or keep an eye on youngsters while they finish homework. For an area that's small in size, it's remarkably big in function.

LOOK BEFORE YOU LEAP →

If an island as big as its namesake is on your agenda of must-have features, you'll need to consider all elements of the design before committing to a gargantuan size. You can certainly build an island as large as your kitchen can accommodate, and it will undoubtedly be a popular gathering spot, but you'll want to source your countertop choice before signing the contract to have the kitchen made. Natural stone slabs of marble and granite are only available up to a certain size, based on the dimensions of the block that was extracted from the quarry. It's wise to double-check the length and

width of the slab you need and ensure you can find one you love before the kitchen is complete. For extra-large measurements, you may find quartz composite counters a better choice, since the material is man-made (using a high percentage of natural quartz mixed with resins), and available in extra-long lengths.

TAKE A BREATHER ↕

A butler's pantry was traditionally built to store large serving pieces used for entertaining, and offered a place to polish the silver away from the main kitchen. Modern-day needs may not necessitate a separate space for your silver to be stored and polished, but having an additional area that can be used as a servery, bar, or staging area when you entertain might be a useful addition to your kitchen. Less-attractive appliances such as the microwave and bar fridge can be tucked away so they don't impact the sight line of beautiful cabinets. And a pantry also offers the opportunity to indulge a distinct colour palette while creating a less formal space. Painting the cabinets in a creamy tone keeps the pantry looking light and bright, which is practical for a room that is often without windows.

THE
FAMILY
ROOM

A distinct family room separate from the main living room is a coveted commodity in real estate transactions, and for good reason. It's the essence of relaxed life at home, since it's where we flock when work, homework, and all the chores are done. As a place for chilling out, snuggling up, tuning in, or just zoning out, your family room should be the magnet that pulls your family close and keeps them connected in an environment that delivers the comfort you crave and the warmth you associate with family life.

SLEEK LOUNGE

We all have diverse lifestyles and different priorities for life at home, and that is what makes the experience of design a unique adventure on each and every project. Family style is not easy to define, as it manifests in so many different forms, but family and style should not be mutually exclusive pursuits. Of course, that includes a home where young children are raised with an appreciation of art and design and are encouraged to both enjoy and respect their environment. This is one of those spaces that is stylish yet comfortable, artful yet approachable.

STICK WITH THE CLASSICS ←

When embarking on the design of a family room, it's never a bad idea to play it safe with colours. If you invest in good-quality pieces of furniture, you'll want them to survive the long haul without appearing outdated, so a neutral palette is always a safe bet. Even if you cover the main investment pieces in the room, such as the chairs and sofa, in durable, hard-wearing textiles, you'll still have plenty of room to infuse colourful accents in your signature palette. You won't likely tire of a classic oyster-toned sofa, but the appeal of that tomato red may start to wane before you are ready for a decorating do-over.

GO FOR BIG IMPACT ←

A family room in an open-concept home with active little kids should be laid out with traffic flow in mind. Being aware of your lifestyle and realistic about the way your family uses every room in the house will help you make the best and most informed choices. My go-to rule for a space like this is to use the smallest number of well-scaled pieces to comfortably furnish the room without making it feel crowded. Design for the number of people who will use the room daily, not the number of people who might visit on occasion (since they will likely all be standing in the adjacent kitchen).

BOLD GESTURES ←

A room based on the principle of well-edited design takes the approach that each and every ingredient in the room matters and needs to add value to the space. Forget cluttering your home with more stuff, and focus on a list of what you really need to pare your furnishings down to a well-curated collection of items you both love and use. In this case, the art above the mantel is high impact and occupies the entire available space with its bold composition, while the floor lamp is similarly large in scale and stands out as the only practical light fixture in the room. Sometimes less is more.

NEUTRAL NEST

The main-floor family room is a high-demand spot in many households that is expected to seamlessly transition from child-friendly play zone (during daylight hours) into adult-friendly lounging and entertaining area (during evenings and weekends). Navigating the fine balance between a place young kids can play independently while still under close supervision from an adjoining room such as the kitchen and making it look like a place that you want to spend time in without feeling as if you're visiting a toy showroom can be challenging. I'm a strong believer that having kids does not go hand in hand with giving up your sense of style and sophistication. I *do* believe that it is possible to have rooms that are not off-limits to kids, yet still look lovely and presentable once their busy little bodies have nodded off to sleep.

___

SPICE UP YOUR NEUTRALS ⇢
A monochromatic palette doesn't need to be a snooze. Take your old beige-on-beige room and update it with shades of grey and tones of camel and caramel. If you're worried about finding a colour scheme that is family friendly, remember this: there is no more forgiving decorating palette than one that is based on the colours of dirt. For added flexibility and easy care, choose an all-cotton upholstery fabric, prewash and predry it before using it for upholstery, and have your seat cushions made without piping, and you'll always be able to wash the seat covers whenever disaster strikes.

KEEP IT LOW ⇢
When you lower your sight line and only install cabinetry on the bottom of the wall, you can put some of the savings toward finishing touches. A honed-granite counter with tones of caramel and charcoal that are drawn from the overall room scheme and high-impact cabinetry hardware that is anything but basic kitchen fare ups the ante on your installation from off the rack to customizable chic. Paying attention to the finishing decorative touches will take your inexpensive storage solution to another level.

GET LOOPY ⇢
Hooked rugs are an iconic country-decor staple and a collectible folk-art form, but they've also made a resurgence in the design market as a practical and hard-wearing construction for wool carpets. Thanks to the short-looped construction, hooked rugs are softer underfoot than a simple flat-woven style, are offered in more interesting patterns than most broadloom options, and don't fuzz or shed as much as tufted versions. Combine all these aspects and you've got a durable and family-friendly choice that's easy to vacuum and easy on the eyes.

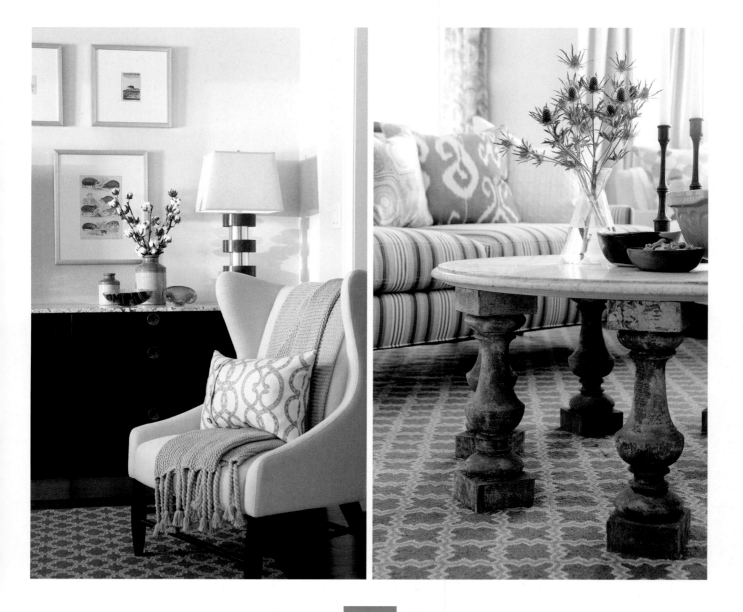

CELEBRATE SALVAGE ➻

Having trouble finding just the right rustic contemporary table to perfectly fit your room? It's easier than you might think to make a one-of-a-kind coffee table using architectural salvage. By attaching reclaimed balusters (originally used as exterior elements on a porch or balcony) to a disc of plywood, you can create a sturdy yet inexpensive base. Top it with a round piece of honed marble and you'll have a durable and fabulous-looking centerpiece in the room (with no sharp edges for running toddlers to crash into, if that's a concern).

POLISHED PENTHOUSE

A family room isn't just a place to flop down and tune in to the tube. If properly appointed, this central gathering room can offer something to every member of the family. Equal parts laid-back lounge, hangout space, TV zone, and flexible work area, this family room may appear poised and polished, but it's really designed for kicking back and connecting.

GAME ON

Whether being used as a spot to read the paper in the morning, work on a laptop, or face off in a friendly match of backgammon, cards, or a board game, a games table adds a multipurpose twist to your family room dynamic. The long, narrow proportions of this room resulted in extra space once the main seating area was laid out, and the placement of another seating area tucked under the window takes advantage of the view beyond.

GET SUITED

With a mix of masculine and feminine influences, this room is designed to appeal to both sexes through an equal balance of details for him and for her. For him, the antique games table has a richly tooled leather top, and the stylized wing chairs are dressed in snappy grey flannel with a windowpane check and finished with a row of polished nickel nail heads to channel a men's club vibe. For her, the windows are dressed in printed linen adorned with a watercolour floral, the walls are painted a delicate powdery blue, and a pretty silver bouillotte lamp sits atop the table.

KNOW YOUR AUDIENCE ←

Precious furniture has no place in a family room, and if you've got a teenage boy, you'll know all too well where their feet inevitably land . . . on the coffee table. To introduce furnishings that satisfy the mandate for kid-friendly chic, go for items that meet your indestructibility criteria. An aluminum side table and riveted, industrial-style steel coffee table add a modern touch and ensure Mom won't freak when those feet find their natural resting spot. A big table also provides ample space for a spread of snacks when entertaining.

LEARN FROM THE PROS ↘

You might regard velvet as a delicate material that's not suited to heavy-duty usage. There are different levels of durability, and you should check the wear rating before you purchase any plush fabric to ensure it won't crush or crease when sat on, but you can rest easy knowing that the seats in theatres were traditionally covered in mohair velvet for its durability and good looks. If you want your family room sofa to look great no matter how much use it gets, I'd suggest you put your money on mohair velvet.

Some rooms seem to call out for sparkle, shine, and glamourous accents, but when a room caters to family life and is filled with natural light, a subdued textural palette strikes the right note. In a family room within an open-concept home, this area links to the adjoining spaces seamlessly thanks to a naturally neutral palette inspired by the sandy shores nearby.

KEEP IT MOVING ←

Arranging furniture in a room that is also a circulation space for the daily flow of traffic through the house can be challenging. To make the best use of the space, you'll need to delineate how traffic should transition through the room without making it feel like an airport terminal. Be sure to leave enough room to pass through without fear of walking into a table or stubbing a toe, and select accent pieces like these wicker tables, which are easy to relocate within the room as needed (and easy on the shins in case you bump into them).

GO WITH THE FLOW ←

In many contemporary houses, boxy silhouettes are the norm, but I like to mix and match basic shapes and play with variations on a theme. Sofas and chairs are generally rectilinear, but you can shake things up with accent pieces. The painting, coffee table, occasional stools, and lamps in this room all reference a circular motif and create a natural sense of flow through the space. With no hard edges, this room feels calm and welcoming.

DON'T GO OVERBOARD ←

The secret to embracing any motif is knowing when to stop. The repetition of the rounded shape in the side tables, coffee table, painting, and lamps is broken up by the grid-patterned carpet, which introduces contrast and helps the room project a more contemporary flavour.

FOLLOW YOUR OWN BEAT ↕

I thrive on creating rooms that are interesting and engaging, and have an element of surprise. Instead of settling for basic accent pieces such as tables, look for unusual objects to incorporate into your decor. A vintage drum turned into a coffee table sets the tone for a mood of casual ease in the family room, while woven stools resembling bobbins double as both cocktail tables and extra seating for a crowd.

KEEP IT SIMPLE ↕

When a casual and comfortable ambiance is on the agenda, you'll want to embrace natural materials with a rustic spirit. The egg-shaped, turned-wood lamps have an elegant silhouette that is rendered in a simple and casual manner to continue the theme of simple elegance.

PLAY WELL WITH OTHERS ↕

When looking for family-friendly fabrics, keep it simple and stick to the basics. Since comfort is the mandate, you'll want to select upholstered furniture profiles that are inviting and comfortable. A traditional chair profile looks clean and classic with a wooden leg instead of a skirt, and light-toned woven fabrics with a subtle pattern keep the room feeling light and airy, yet help hide the wear and tear of daily use.

RELAXED REC ROOM

The rec room has come a *long* way since I was a child. In the '70s our play spaces often had a slight whiff of mildew and felt more dungeonlike than divine. Think concrete floors, painted brick walls, and the occasional piece of discarded furniture draped with a blanket. In the 21st century, as house prices soar skyward, we're all looking to make the most of every square inch we have available, and that includes the basement. By focusing on furnishings that are both practical and inviting, and adding interest with colour, fabrics, and paint, you can easily make your basement a destination that's every bit as chic and appealing as every other room.

MAKE A MIX ↣
Outfitting an oversized room in fully upholstered furnishings can become expensive pretty quickly, so keep your eyes open for vintage pieces at bargain prices that can help extend your budget (and prevent the room from feeling too heavy and similar in style). These vintage open armchairs were transformed thanks to fresh paint and a peppy paisley print. With a plush back cushion they're comfortable too, and the airy frames keep the light streaming in from the window behind.

START FROM THE GROUND UP ↣
Subterranean spaces aren't known for emitting a warm and cozy vibe, but that's easily altered if you start your room planning with colourful and plush rugs underfoot. While Persian carpets are often regarded as traditional looking, I think a Heriz carpet is a wonderful way to bring vibrant colour and a vividly graphic pattern to a room. The dense pattern and overall colour is also forgiving for family life (stain . . . what stain?).

PLAN FOR LAID-BACK LIVING ↣
Some rooms require us to be on our best behaviour, while others provide a place to kick back and put our feet up. This is it! When it comes to the right table, I like a timeworn treasure with some patina that invites you to put your feet up and doesn't require coasters or caution when the snacks are served. An antique pine worktable can easily be altered to your desired height and provides an expansive coffee table surface.

GENTLEMEN'S QUARTERS ↕

The rec room is often the domain of the boys, so why not add a man-cave
nod to the decor? I still like a room that works for both sexes, so a blend of
grey flannel upholstery and windowpane-check pillows gives a nod to menswear
influences, while an oversized block-printed floral gives a softer touch.

ACCENT, DON'T OVERPOWER ↕
A large-scale room offers ample opportunity to embrace colour,
but it needn't be all encompassing. If you "bookend" opposite end walls
by painting them an intense hue, it helps shrink the distance in between
and unifies the space. Keep the side walls in a neutral tone (such as grey),
and the overall feeling will be both light and impactful.

THE
BEDROOM

Your bedroom should be a place to surround yourself with elements that make you feel calm at the end of a long day and allow you to rise feeling rested and ready to tackle the world yet again. So, what's your boudoir style? Is it cozy and comfy, romantic and rich? Or streamlined and minimalist, contemporary and chic? Whether you crave a bedroom that is luxuriously appointed in opulent textures or sparingly adorned in sleek lines, knowing your bedroom preferences and style will help you create the ultimate sanctuary of rest and relaxation.

LUXURY SUITE

A big challenge with newly built houses such as this one is that they can be completely lacking in personality. I wanted this large bedroom to be a refuge for the homeowners, who are busy professionals with four little girls. I layered luxury at every level to create a sumptuous experience that would provide an air of softness, calm, and relaxation and went for a cultivated mix of new and old, rather than a one-stop shop for a bedroom suite. Forget mix and match, this room is all about "mix and mix."

MASTER THE MIX ↪
When designing your master bedroom, be sure to blend a variety of influences to achieve an eclectic mix. This bedroom retreat brings a soothing, neutral palette to life thanks to a rich layering of textures. Hammered metal, lacquered wood, patterned damask wallpaper, quilted textiles, luminescent silk, and glowing alabaster guarantees that "restrained" can still be remarkable.

MAKE IT PERSONAL ↗
Not every bedroom can accommodate multiple seating areas, but many small-scale rooms can accommodate some sort of chair-and-table configuration. When selecting furniture for a bedroom, remember this is a private space, not one for entertaining. A pair of streamlined klismos-inspired chairs with graceful proportions flank a hammered-nickel table, providing a practical and elegant perch without occupying too much floor space.

CREATE A GLOW ↗
Whenever possible, I like to splurge on lighting. A ceiling this ornate deserves more than pot lights and demands a fixture worthy of its detailing, such as this hand-painted Fortuny lamp. When in doubt about lighting, turn it up a notch and get the best you can afford. You won't likely regret investing in great lighting. It sets the mood and makes everyone look good.

LOOK UP! ↗
Any bland builder's box of a home can be infused with old-world glamour thanks to master-craftsman details. Adding an intricate "wedding cake" plaster fretwork and crown moulding to an oversized master bedroom took it from grand proportion to glam style without a major renovation.

PILLOW TALK

Decorative accents and custom pillows offer the perfect opportunity to introduce an out-of-the-ordinary colour palette. You might shy away from lavender, mustard, and oyster as an overall room scheme, but that doesn't mean you need to pass up on experimenting with these favourite hues in small doses.

GO FOR HANDMADE

The traditional pattern of damask wallpaper appears more contemporary when rendered in a large-scale, tone-on-tone palette. When splurging on wallpaper for a single-wall installation, take your cues for the wall colour from the paper, and match the rest of the room to the wallpaper's background colour. By selecting a uniform backdrop, the pattern will appear as though it were applied by hand. This is an especially easy effect to achieve when working with hand-blocked paper that is rich with texture.

BRING LUXURY HOME

An upholstered headboard and side rails give this king-sized bed a streamlined appeal while reinforcing that a beautifully made bed is an attainable luxury. A trio of generously sized silk pillows with a pair of petite accent pillows tops the bed with a plush touch and fulfills the five-star pampering quotient. When working with a neutral palette, you can infuse subtle touches of colour such as lilac and gold to reinforce the room's restrained opulence.

TREAD SOFTLY

This grid-patterned, hand-knotted Tibetan area rug in oyster grey introduces softness underfoot and acts as a contrast to the intricate pattern of the ceiling above. When placing an area rug in a bedroom, I prefer to have two bed legs on the rug and two legs off, as opposed to tucking the entire rug up under the bed, so more carpet is left in the seating area of the room.

OPPOSITES ATTRACT ⟂

Keep the tension alive by contrasting influences and tones.
A plush, tufted side chair is offset by a subdued grid carpet;
a heavy, dark credenza gets a lift from a pale silver-leafed mirror;
and crystal lamps with silky shades stand beside stark black-
and-white images. Thanks to a fusion of masculine and feminine
elements, this bedroom has something to offer both him
and her.

EMBRACE YOUR OPTIONS ↕

Evaluate your need for storage in the bedroom and explore
options beyond a generic chest of drawers. This Indonesian
black-lacquered credenza wouldn't normally be considered a
go-to bedroom piece, but here it provides storage for TV components and clothes, while its long and low proportion balances the
shape of the daybed and its glossy finish plays up the ebonized
trim of the klismos-inspired chairs.

MAXIMIZE YOUR ASSETS ↕

Placing a tall mirror perpendicular to a low storage unit allows the
long, low surface to be treated as a dressing table while emphasizing the height of the ceilings.

BE A DAYDREAMER ↕

When deciding on furniture for a bay window, consider which
vantage point you want to enjoy. Placing chairs or a sofa in
this bay window would impede the view while shifting the
sight lines to face into the room, but a daybed creates an
unobstructed view to the ravine beyond with flexibility to
focus on whatever tickles your fancy.

FRACTIONAL RELATIONS ↕

Generally, I like to position the curtain rod halfway between the
top of the window trim and the bottom of the crown moulding. This placement fills the void between the two spaces and
gives breathing space to the bay window.

SERENE ESCAPE

While some rooms in your home are designed for gathering and sharing, your bedroom offers refuge and a quiet, private getaway from the outside world. When faced with the challenge of bringing spirit and soul to a bland, oversized box of a bedroom, I relied on a light and airy garden palette to create a restful retreat that brings the glory of spring indoors.

THE FRAME-UP ↣
Add impact to a bland wall by installing a simple and inexpensive trim profile to create an oversized panel, then apply decorative wallpaper to the interior of the panel. It's easier to install wallpaper in a smaller area, and since you'll need less to achieve the effect, you'll save money too. I jump at any opportunity to layer colour and patterns together, so this tactic is a winning strategy in my book.

GET INTO THE SWING ↣
If drama is what you're after, try juxtaposing overscaled swing-arm lamps with more traditionally styled bedside tables. The height of the lamps helps balance the tall headboard, while the buttery tone of the painted tables reinforces the light and airy mood of the overall scheme.

GO BACK IN TIME

Embrace the theme of old meets new by integrating as much vintage furniture as possible into the mix to give a new home some much-needed soul. You can reinforce your chosen accent colour by introducing it in vases, bowls, lamps, and small accessories. I am constantly on the lookout for vintage items and often find that the quality and the price is better than what you find in new products.

SET YOUR SIGHTS ⬂

Design your room with a view in mind. If space permits, why not introduce a writing desk to your master suite that allows you to gaze out the window while you tackle your daily correspondence or catch up on unfinished business? I scooped up a vintage '70s linen-covered desk for a deal and gave it a contemporary update with a new walnut base and modern drawer knobs.

PLAN TO PERCH ⬂

Since you won't likely be seated for extended stints at a bedroom desk, it makes sense to choose a pretty perch with a light, lyrical look and an open back that won't appear too dense when seen from behind. A tie-on chair pad adds a soft touch and is a good way to make use of remnant fabric from the headboard.

LAYER ON PATTERN ↕

Strike up a pretty palette with a variety of fabrics. A wide tent stripe on a tall and curvaceous headboard creates the illusion of height in a room (even if it only has standard 8-foot ceilings), while a graphic weave, a monochromatic floral, and a peach-toned wool gabardine top a quilted bedspread to add layers of luxury and plenty of texture to the bed. The combination of geometric, floral, and textural patterns is an effective way to marry traditional and contemporary style influences in a room.

EMBELLISH THE ARCHITECTURE ↤

If your home is lacking architectural interest, buy it! Architectural salvage is a green way to add character, charm, and patina to a new home. These exterior Ionic columns were the exact height of the ceilings and help frame a subtle definition of spaces in an oversized bedroom. If you find columns that are too tall for your ceilings, you might be able to reduce the overall height by cutting down the shaft portion between the base and the capital.

COSMOPOLITAN SUITE

One of the delights of checking into a modern boutique hotel is the atmosphere of calm and quiet that pervades above a bustling city street below. But why should you have to leave home to experience the chic contemporary style you associate with a hotel when you can infuse your own bedroom with a cool cosmopolitan vibe? This tired high-rise condo was given a new lease on life with plush finishes and a subdued masculine palette that acts as an antidote to busy urban life.

FIND YOUR STARTING POINT ←
Every room starts with a jumping-off point that helps define the overall direction of the design. A pair of vintage George Nelson side tables acted as the foundation from which all other choices were influenced in this bedroom. The grid pattern of the drawers is referenced in the menswear-inspired wool windowpane check on the tailored headboard, and the light/dark mix was repeated on the drapes, accent fabrics, and in the boldly striped broadloom that anchors the space. The horizontal framed artwork echoes the shape of the side table, with the green grass in the image complementing the bright green lamp and the open road adding depth to the space.

MAKE IT LIKE A LATTE

This bedroom could be likened to the way many of us start each and
every day — with a shot of espresso in a mug full of milk. The palette is
a comforting range of cozy latte-toned neutrals, in everything from the
walls to the fabrics and floor coverings. When creating a space with
a warm, modern vibe, rich chocolate and coffee present a perfect pairing.

TAKE YOUR LIGHTING TO TASK ⬍

There are no rules about what style of lighting you need to use in particular areas of your home, and your selection of style should be a matter of personal choice. Often overlooked as strictly office-appropriate, the flexible task light is a favourite bedside illuminator for me. Sleek and streamlined, a task lamp will enable you to focus a beam of light on the page you're reading without illuminating the entire room and waking your bedmate.

—

DRAW IT OUT ↘

After laying the groundwork for a scheme in a monochromatic palette, I look to inject an accent colour to enliven and energize the finished space. You can seek inspiration anywhere, but in this room, a piece of art from the client's collection offered ample opportunity to extract a high-intensity hue. The bold kelly green in the painting is echoed in the cheetah-print linen on the bed pillows, in the lamps, and in a few vintage accessories throughout the room.

REGAL OASIS

With three tiny kids underfoot, the owners of this bedroom were more familiar with sleepless nights than uninterrupted quiet. After buying their "lifetime" home for its great bones and coveted neighbourhood, they found themselves camped out in a bland and unadorned master bedroom that was outfitted with a mishmash of furniture they'd accumulated along the way. What they craved was a bedroom that seemed as "grown-up" as their house. So I created a calm and sophisticated refuge from the sea of kid stuff that had overtaken the rest of their home, and a space that would be theirs alone.

COOL SHADES ←

Panelled walls offer an easy opportunity to play with a multihued paint scheme. Using the predominant shades of dark and light grey for the areas above and below the chair rail creates a harmonious connection to the room's fabric scheme, and the ceiling is the ideal place to introduce a subtle hint of colour by reinforcing the accent blues. After all, a pale blue ceiling is far more inspiring to wake up to than plain old white.

PAINT ←

When choosing paint colours for your bedroom, consider the times of day you are most likely to have the chance to spend time enjoying your environs. If your bedroom is painted in a deep, smoky hue, it will feel inviting in the evening, and you might just find yourself stealing away to curl up with a good book rather than turning on the TV.

CHANNEL HOTEL STYLE ←

When the goal of redesigning your bedroom is to create a tranquil refuge from the busy world on the other side of the door, it logically follows that you might benefit from borrowing a page from the amenities of luxury hotels. There's always a chair (or two) just waiting for you to collapse in after a long day on your feet, ample storage to absorb all your stuff, a delightfully plush bed, and a desk area to serve as mission control. In essence, it's got everything you need, so when space permits, I suggest you go for the gusto and outfit your bedroom with everything you'd expect to find in a five-star hotel.

THE FRAME-UP ➻

For a better-than-average look, consider layering your window treatments. I started with a gauzy Roman blind made from inexpensive and lightweight printed Indian cotton for privacy, then added a layer of full-length drapes for drama. These wide-striped dupioni silk drapes were added to frame up the view and amp up the glam factor with a hint of sheen!

HEAD FOR THE WOODS ➻

For every part of a room that is fresh and new, I tend to counter it with another element that has history and soul. While there are many options for new, wood-case good furnishings, I've always found that more unique and inspiring spaces are created by introducing vintage and antique finds. The footstool is light enough to slide back and forth and serve as a footrest for both chairs; the side table has a generous surface to accommodate a lamp, books, and even a tea tray; and the pale marble top on the console offsets the richness of the antique walnut and mahogany woods. I like to think of these accent furniture pieces like the accessories you add to an outfit—each should have the presence and personality to make a statement.

SING THE BLUES ➚

Look for inexpensive art glass baubles, paperweights, and bowls (or ashtrays) at consignment shops and flea markets. They're a great way to introduce an additional hit of your accent colour, and the bowls make handy catchalls for pocket change or jewellery.

FLOOR-TO-CEILING WOW ←

Bookshelves need not be a dull, uniform visual statement. If you're short on books to fill all the shelves, experiment with ways to make the most effective use of the space. This wall was originally built with a deeper centre cabinet to hold the TV, but since it's no longer needed, the area was reimagined into a pretty dressing table, and the bookshelves were adjusted to allow room for antique etchings, books, and a slim-profile TV. To add more impact to your installation, paint the back wall of your bookshelves in a darker colour (such as the deep gray-green wall colour used in this bedroom), and paint the frames and shelves in trim paint.

ROOM WITH A VIEW ↕

Take advantage of outside views and tuck a writing desk into an alcove so you can work near the light and gaze through the treetops. Many of us only work on a laptop (or tablet) at home, so you may not need a big desk with lots of storage. Having a little desk in the bedroom provides a quiet spot away from the buzz of the house in a tranquil environment.

CREATE A CONNECTION ↕

Connect your bedroom to your en suite bath by continuing the colour scheme, but experiment with variations on a theme so it feels as though it flows, but doesn't "match." Dress up a plain white vanity by repainting the doors and adding new hardware in a finish that connects to the bedroom. Instead of shiny chrome or nickel for the faucets and lighting, try incorporating a darker metal tone such as oil-rubbed bronze. Since this sink is located in the dressing area of the closet and is away from the steam in the shower, I chose to add classic-tent stripe wallpaper for this patterned effect.

MODERN MINIMALISM

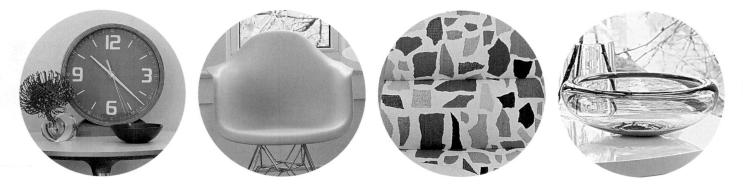

There's no one "correct" vision for outfitting your nest, but there's definitely a compelling argument for embracing the "less is more" aesthetic when it comes to decorating your bedroom, especially when balancing style with the need for organization in tight city quarters. Capacious walk-in closets and floor plans with plenty of room to roam are certainly not de rigueur in the average downtown home, so you need to redefine what's really necessary in a "master" bedroom. It may not always be grand—but it can always be great!

START FROM SCRATCH ←

Whether you're executing a dramatic overhaul or just doing some minor redecoration, the best way to achieve a divinely dreamy master bedroom is to move everything out of the room and start with a blank slate. I guarantee that if you take everything out, then evaluate, one at a time, whether you want to reintroduce each item, you will soon have a rather large haul to donate to charity. Don't wait for spring to reevaluate what you're stashing in your bedroom; the time to purge is now . . . and often.

CHANNEL A CLASSIC ←

You may not want to dedicate precious space to a big bed frame, but a sleek and simple wall-mounted headboard will give the bed structure and contribute to the room's decor. Inspired by the channel-back profile of a classic Marcel Breuer midcentury chair

with upholstery detail, this headboard is tailored yet tactile and brings a bit of fun and colour to the mix. While you may want to keep all of the main elements in the room streamlined and sparse, a headboard is the ideal place to experiment with pattern and colour. This jaunty modern textile has a groovy vibe and makes an ideal cover for it!

MAKE YOUR OWN RULES ←

Who says your bedside light needs to sit on a table? If you're tight on space, consider installing pendant lights that hang from the ceiling instead of devoting precious room on your nightstand table to a reading lamp. When house rules dictate sleek and modern style, a pared-down hanging light may be just the right night-light.

STORE BEFORE YOU STYLE

Closets aren't always the first priority when approaching a design scheme, but if you're living in a home that is spatially challenged for closets, you'll need to devise solutions to keep the clutter at bay. Old city houses are famous for having minuscule closets of inadequate depth, which proves problematic for many a clothes-horse. The simple solution in this not-so-grand master bedroom was to install his and hers L-shaped, floor-to-ceiling closet systems on either side of the bay window for maximum customized storage with minimal visual clutter. With an efficient mix of folded and hanging storage, even the smallest spaces can have a "place for everything, and everything in its place." By committing to adequate square footage to keep your haven organized, you'll be able to assess the leftover space and prioritize what's needed versus what's nice to have.

CHOOSE PEDIGREE OVER PLUSH

An upholstered bedroom chair brings texture, colour, and pattern to a bedroom (and serves as a pit stop for things you aren't quite ready to hang up . . .). If you've got a compact space, a chair that offers sculptural interest and a hit of colour without occupying too much space might be the right solution. Here, a compact bay window even offers enough room for a multipurpose table for you and your better half!

EXPECT MORE ⬍

Thanks to the growing number of city dwellers living in small spaces, furniture design is evolving in multifunctional ways. Before you sign up for a run-of-the-mill box spring as the "foundation" of your mattress, why not consider a solution that does double duty? Replace that old-school box spring with a stylish yet inexpenisve storage bed base with numerous ample-sized drawers.

BREAK DOWN BARRIERS ⬍

Old houses are constructed of lath-and-plaster walls, but there are other solutions tc bring a light, bright touch to your home. Instead of rebuilding relocated walls in the standard stud-and-drywall construction, consider alternate materials that save space and add style. Instead of drywall, we installed panels of tempered glass, then covered them with vinyl adhesive that was digitally printed from a contemporary photograph. The glass panels are installed to stay, but the vinyl art can be peeled off and changed whenever the urge to redecorate strikes!

PARISIAN BOUDOIR

In an upper-level bedroom where the afternoon sunlight comes streaming in, a palette of glorious and bright garden-inspired pink and purple hues mingle together to present a grown-up take that proves pretty and pink isn't just for dollhouses and baby girls' rooms.

ROLL OUT THE RIBBON ←•

When browsing through flea markets and consignment shops, I can't resist picking up small antique or vintage footstools, as they are a flexible and useful accent piece in almost any room. Whether placed in front of a chair in the bedroom to invite you to put your feet up, or tucked beneath a dressing table as a place to perch while you put the finishing touches on your look, or scattered in a living room to act as both a rest for weary feet and extra seating for a crowd, footstools are a flexible and indispensable element in every space. You'll likely find these vintage gems for a bargain price, covered in awfully dated fabric, but since you'll need less than a yard of fabric to transform them, you can create a small but stylish showpiece. If the appropriate fabric for your chosen colour scheme can't be found, head for the trim department at the fabric store and embellish a piece of plain fabric with a basket-weave application of grosgrain ribbons that are sewn in place before the stool gets reupholstered.

APPRECIATE THE ARMOIRE ←•

Not every bedroom has ample closet space, and some have none, so the easy solution to your storage woes is to buy an antique armoire that was originally designed to accommodate both hanging and folded clothes. The faux bamboo embellishments and mirrored door on this antique piece add far more presence than any drywall closet ever could, and if you move, you'll be able to take it with you.

KNOW WHEN TO STOP ←•

Having the courage to play with bold colour is terrific, and knowing when to pull back on the reins is invaluable. In order for the colourful elements to seem like interesting and unique moments, some breathing space is required, so instead of splashing your bright and cheery palette on every imaginable surface, leave some white space to fill the gaps. In this room, the walls are washed in barely there pink, and the chairs, bed linens, and skirt are pure white and natural linen to prevent pattern overload.

HANG IT ON THE WALL ↕

If you are tight on space and have diminutive bedside tables, you might
want to consider installing sconces on the wall, centred above each
nightstand, to illuminate your bedtime book while still leaving space
for necessities on the tabletop. If you select sconces that are hardwired
and need a wall switch to turn on or off, you can usually have
a discreet toggle switch added to the backplate so you'll be able
to switch them on and off without lifting your head from the pillow.

CURATE A COLLECTION ↕

It's the little details that can make a big statement and add an element of fun to your shopping adventures. When shopping for finishing touches, I tend to seek out vintage smalls. They are generally priced comparably or even more economically than any new accessory, yet are better quality and have inherent value due to their age and origin. Shop around, and before you know, you'll have a lovely collection of art glass to use, display, and enjoy.

DRAW AN OUTLINE ↕

Even the simplest window coverings can have a layered mix of colour and pattern. Tailored Roman blinds made from creamy linen with a delicate embroidered floral motif are given a preppy update with a band of polka-dot ribbon sewn around the perimeter.

ATTIC GUEST QUARTERS

The ideal guest room can be carved out in any area, whether big or small, to offer a comforting and relaxing home away from home for friends and family. Tucked up on the third floor of a downtown Edwardian house, this compact guest room is packed with charm and character and feels like a tree house with its sloped ceiling and leafy location amidst a canopy of mature trees. Be forewarned: when you have a desirable destination, reservations fill up fast!

PLAN AHEAD ↤

When visualizing a new project, you must consider how it will feel in every season. Air-conditioning and climate-control systems aside, it's just sensible to be aware of how your house heats or cools depending on the weather so you can tailor your selections of materials to work in all four seasons. The connection to the outdoors was undeniably strong in this room, so the fabrics, carpet, and accessories were all chosen to mimic the leaf-meets-sky palette that is always visible through the narrow French doors.

GONE COUNTRY ↧

If your goal is to make your guests feel at ease, the country-style vernacular is brimming with inspiration to help you achieve the look of laid-back chic even in the most urban locations. With a hooked rug, an antique quilt, and cool cotton fabrics, this room is sure to put guests at ease and make them feel welcome. To appease both sexes, consider mixing menswear plaid and herringbone with delicately carved alabaster lamps and a sweet antique quilt. The subdued colour scheme of muted olives, greens, and smoky grey is neither too feminine nor too masculine.

FORMAL FLAT

Feathering your nest and decorating your bedroom should be a voyage destined to showcase your personal style. After all, your bedroom isn't for receiving guests or catering to family, it's where you retreat to rest and recharge each day. The personal investment is what makes each bedroom uniquely suited to its inhabitants, and in this case my client wanted a traditionally appointed space filled with luxurious amenities and intricate detail.

PICK YOUR PERCH ←
Chairs come in many shapes and sizes, from tiny to gigantic. Your bedroom may not be grand enough to accommodate a giant upholstered armchair, but that doesn't mean you need to go without some soft seating in your private escape. Although compact in proportions, these Louis XV chairs are long on comfort thanks to a padded back and down-filled seat. If you are considering adding a pair of chairs to the foot of your bed, be on the lookout for a style with a rounded-back profile, as it will occupy less space in the room and create a soft line when tucked in with a petite table.

PLAY A SUPPORTING ROLE ←
When designing a room, I aim to curate a collection of elements that range from ornamental to ordinary. If everything you introduce in a room is a showstopping element, no single aspect will seem special, and the cumulative effect may be overwhelming. After selecting an antique mahogany bed and side tables with ormolu details and decorative veneers, there were clearly enough stars of the show. By using solid and printed linen as a humble contrast to ornate furnishings, you can celebrate the simple beauty of natural materials and create a room that is elegant without being ostentatious.

MAKE IT YOUR MOMENT ←

The unique combination of handblown Murano glass lighting, an antique French parquetry dressing table, and an ornate English silver mirror forms an eclectic yet personal expression of style in this bedroom. If you fill the rooms in your home with individual pieces that appeal to you, you can be guaranteed to have a home unlike any other, and one that is your personal oasis.

KEEP IT LEAN ↕

When searching for just the right lamp to pair with your bedside tables, you'll want to achieve balance and harmony. Sleek and slender tables like these would be overwhelmed by a bulbous lamp base, and the top would be completely consumed, so it's best to pair a tailored table with an equally elegant lamp. Always make sure you try your tables and lamps together before you deem them a match made in heaven.

FOLLOW THE RULES ↕

A number of factors will determine if your lamp is the right height for your bed, but generally speaking, the beam of light projecting from the base of the lampshade should fall on the page of whatever you are reading in bed. If you keep the top of your lamps roughly level with the top of your headboard, you will have achieved the right balance of heights for both side tables and lamps. But like any good recipe, you can adjust the suggested measurements to find the right mix for your taste.

BACHELOR LOFT

Redecorating a bachelor pad is a task rife with stereotypes and macho themes. Immediately, one conjures up images of black leather, chrome, giant TVs, and stereo equipment stacked to the ceiling. It can be tricky to steer clear of all these connotations and arrive at a fresh, intelligent approach to the challenge of designing a home for the modern single man. With the goal of designing a space that was more gentleman's quarters than macho bachelor pad, I focused on harnessing the energetic spirit and unbridled enthusiasm of my client to arrive at a room that is unique and unconventional.

CUSTOM BED ↤

This loft space had an undeniable cool factor thanks to its former use as a baseball-glove factory. Immediately, this would be a draw for any single, sports-loving guy and might provide ample inspiration for design motifs. But instead of going hog wild with an all-star sports vibe, I embraced the baseball legacy quietly and discreetly. After designing a custom bed, covered in daring dragon fabric, we opted to use distressed brown leather (reminiscent of a baseball glove) on the side rails. It's practical and durable but manly — no jerseys, no gloves, no bats needed.

INDUSTRIAL FURNISHINGS ↤

When furnishing a loft space, be sure to seek out unique and un-usual elements that add warmth. Instead of opting for run-of-the-mill "modern" and big, boxy furnishings, introduce accents with a story that tells a past history. A pair of industrial shop tables can be repurposed as stools at the foot of the bed, a vintage ladder creates a whimsical play on scale, and a pair of tire moulds can be turned into showstopping mirrors. When balanced with an equivalent infusion of finer furnishings, these rough-and-ready elements add patina and keep the mood youthful and fun.

KEEP YOUR OPTIONS OPEN ⬍
Some think that open-concept homes limit the options for multiple paint colours.
I do not subscribe to that opinion, and enjoy experimenting with various hues.
When I enter a home, I like to see one room juxtaposed against the next and enjoy
the play of layered colours within a single sight line. Even if your home doesn't have
distinct "rooms" defined by doors and trim, I heartily encourage you to mix
it up — avoid the temptation to keep it all consistent. Any corner is an opportunity
to break from one hue to another. It's easier to paint the inside corner, but if you've
got a steady hand, feel free to cut the line on the outside edge too. Think of the
fun you can have when creating blocks of colour as opposed to a monotone!

COVER UP ⬍
Not every home is a lifetime purchase. A one-bedroom loft is good for a while — an opportunity not to be missed if you can swing it (I lived in two of them and savoured every
moment of my downtown hipster days) — but it's also the type of space that you may
grow out of in time. When considering where to put your decorating dollars, it makes the
most sense to be frugal on any fixings that you cannot take to your next domicile. And
when the job calls for about 60 yards of fabric to dress the windows, you can bet I'm hit-
ting the bargain bins to add softness and texture to the room. If you've got tall windows,
selecting a neutral fabric will allow you to repurpose your window coverings in another
home in the future (or sell them to the new owner when the time comes to move on).

PATTERN PLAY ↕

Don't be afraid of the P-word. *P* is for "pattern," but it doesn't need to be defined as floral, cutesy, and feminine, and it definitely doesn't need to be avoided by all bachelors along with the M-word (marriage). I think pattern brings interest and excitement, dynamism and colour, to any room, and it would be a missed opportunity to forgo it altogether. The jumping-off point that got the creative juices flowing was a bold dragon-print fabric featuring saturated hues of turquoise, teal, red, and ochre. Not all clients want a bedroom that is peppered with primary tones, but my client had said he wanted "POW!" so that's exactly what we tried to deliver.

TABLE TALK ↕

Finding just the right bedside table with the features you desire at the size you need can be a bit of a scavenger hunt. I find that the combination of a drawer and a shelf offers the right balance of open and closed storage. As a rule, look for a bedside table that is about the same height as the top of your mattress so everything is within easy reach.

CHAIR TABLE LAMP ←

A spacious bedroom invites bold gestures. If you've already embraced one strong pattern in the room, you can balance it with a complementary geometric print. The circular motif is reminiscent of gears to underscore the industrial accents, while the colour palette reflects the teal-and-cream combination of the window coverings. The vintage wing chair is a modern interpretation of the traditional profile, which prevents it from feeling old-fashioned, and its height anchors the corner it occupies and makes a bold statement in combination with the machine-age chrome lamp and chunky, painted column table.

LAY IT DOWN ↕

The modern man can't be all hard edges, and neither can his home. A polished concrete floor presents an aura of undeniable hipness, but by layering a luxurious semi-antique Persian carpet over the industrial concrete, you can temper your cool with some warmth. The caveat here is that big spaces demand large floor coverings, so if you're warming it up, you need to do it right and select a carpet that is proportionate to the size of your space. This large carpet can easily be relocated to another home and will retain its value as it continues to age (which is not the case with a newly made option).

CREAMY COMFORT

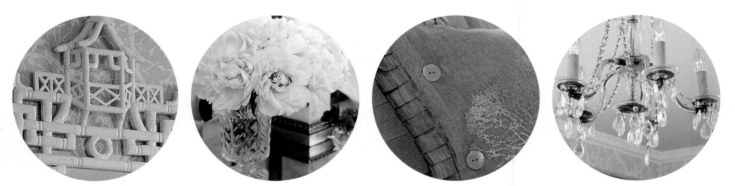

While I'm not afraid of embracing colour and pattern for maximum impact and effect, sometimes a tone-on-tone, neutral scheme is just what the doctor ordered. While I love to play with new ideas and experiment with fresh colour combinations, I fully understand the comfort and sensibility of playing it safe with timeless style choices. If daring and edgy design schemes are your idea of scary, then I suggest you stick with the classics, dress your room in the never-fade glory of silvery-light neutrals, and sleep easy knowing that you won't need to revamp anytime soon!

BE A BARGAIN HUNTER ➻
Great style doesn't have to come with a high price tag—there are always deals to be had! But here's the trick: the best bargains usually come with a challenge. To reap the savings, you'll need to be able to look beyond the flaws, and this is where your imagination needs to kick in. After all, if it were in "take me home," perfect condition, the price tag would no longer seem so appealing, would it? Call me an optimist, but it's the rags-to-riches, ugly-duckling-to-elegant-swan effect that always gets me when I'm combing my favourite haunts for vintage treasures. I challenge myself to dream up how I could make a certain piece better with a coat of paint, some fresh upholstery, and a healthy dose of TLC. The mirrors, side tables, bed, and bench chairs all benefitted from a royal revamp and bear little resemblance to their former state.

TREAT YOURSELF ➻
Every room that is built on good deals benefits from a few special touches to elevate the finished room beyond garage-sale chic. A feature wall of wallpaper is a popular choice to make a bold statement on one wall, but in this case I felt more was more. If you're working in a quiet palette, you can surround yourself in an all-over treatment of delicate pattern without overpowering the room. With a fibrous texture reminiscent of a paper bag and a block-printed white-branch pattern, the effect is evocative of a woodland dreamscape.

BREAK THE RULES ➻
Some say never put the bed under the window. I say put the bed wherever it looks best and maximizes floor space. My rule is that if the rules of design aren't working for you . . . break them! This window is nothing special and has a sill that's too high for my liking, so the goal was to dress around the window to create a better visual statement. The current placement draws you in to the view of the bed and the sky beyond, and the entire vista is surrounded by softly pleated drapes.

LAY ON THE LINEN ⬆

Once you've decided to go natural and neutral, you might as well go the distance and incorporate a healthy dose of my all-time favourite colourless standby — linen. The nubbly weave, earthy texture, and enduring appeal of pure linen infuses luxury and sophistication in an understated fashion. It looks better wrinkled and comes in varying weights from handkerchief to heavy. For this room I combined a number of styles, including linen stitched with a whimsical motif of a bird's footprint, embroidered with trees, and embellished with polka dots. With a little extra attention to detail, basic linen becomes anything but boring.

SCORE ON SAVINGS ⬆

Everything in this room was a deal, but a few real steals certainly helped pull off champagne style on a beer budget. The bench at the foot of the bed was a definite garage-sale bargain (and was no beauty), but thanks to a fresh coat of shiny white paint and reupholstered embroidered linen inserts, this ugly duckling became a functional and fresh addition to the room. The headboard was equally economical and got the same treatment as the bench. With a touch of paint, a bit of fabric . . . voilà, you've got a luxe look for less!

FORGET SYMMETRY ↘

I embrace a certain amount of symmetry in everything I design, but then I need to let other areas be more unexpected and unstructured. There's no rule that says your mirror must be centred above your dresser. When working with a long dresser, I prefer to hang the mirror off to one side. This offset placement allows you to dress one side of the piece with storage accessories and accents, while keeping the other side pristine with just the mirror in place for practical purposes.

—

REAP THE REWARDS ←

Every room has its limitations. One advantage of rejigging your current furniture plan is that you may be able to fit more wish-list items into your room. After relocating the bed, I managed to sneak a pair of lounge chairs into the room, fulfilling the goal of adding comfort and plush touches to the overall scheme.

—

GIVE IT A WASH ←

Next time you're debating which shade of brown to choose for your hardwood floors, why not go in an altogether different direction? Forget trying to mimic mahogany or walnut, and take a page from the greyed or whitewashed tones of the Gustavian influence. I was aiming for a room that would be serene, restorative, and whisper-soft on all surfaces, so I deliberately shied away from any dark-wood accents. The floors were inexpensive to refinish, yet look brand-new! Thinking of trying a whitewash technique at home? When selecting the right stain tone, I suggest you choose a colour with a touch of grey in it for a bleached or pickled look. Trust me, I speak from experience here — if you apply white stain over a red-oak floor, you get . . . peach!

GABLED GETAWAY

When designating an area of your home to be used as a welcoming retreat for guests, you'll want to outfit it in a way that is neither too masculine nor too feminine and suited to visitors of all ages. In a top-floor guest room of a historic town house with a revolving roster of international travellers both young and old, the focus here was on providing a serene spot to sleep off the jet lag and wake up ready to explore the city.

MIX IT UP ⬍
Blending a diverse assortment of patterns that includes stripes and plaid with damask and paisley can seem like an unusual combination, but this lighthearted approach to layering patterns results in an atmosphere of casual elegance that is appealing to all. Choose fabrics in a uniform range of colours that read as neither too juvenile nor too mature.

SEEING DOUBLE ⇥
If symmetry and order appeal to your sense of balance, twin beds are undoubtedly on your list of likes. Many people think that bigger is better in furniture these days, so it's easy to snag a beautiful pair of antique twin beds for less than you'd pay for a mass-produced new version. The old ones are guaranteed to outscore the new models in quality, design, and value.

SHARE FAIRLY ⇥
When working with a pair of twin beds, you may find that two nightstands aren't necessarily better than one. In this case, the sloped walls indicated that it would be best to leave ample room as a corridor between the two beds, so a wide, low table was chosen to connect the beds with a single lamp to illuminate.

MAKE A MIRROR IMAGE ⇥
To play up the symmetry of the bed placement, a tall, gilded mirror hangs centred above the shared bedside table and provides contrast to the low horizontal line of the beds and table. It is also a practical location for a dressing mirror. Instead of art, you can look for unusual objects to hang on the walls, such as these vintage convex porthole mirrors.

BRING THE OUTDOORS IN ↘
The softened palette of muted greens is drawn from the moss that grows on the buttressed stone walls running in front of the windows in this bedroom. If you are looking to connect your home to its surroundings, spend some time gazing out the windows as you look for a sign to influence your design.

ENCOURAGE ORDER ⬍
While you may not want your guests to get too comfortable and overstay their welcome, it's important to provide a place to unpack so they can keep organized and enjoy the well-appointed surroundings you've provided them. A black-painted dresser covered with découpaged fish has enough drawers to store extra bedding and supplies while still leaving a few drawers free for visitors' belongings. A desk with a lamp and a chair is another thoughtful addition to your furniture plan that enables your guests to enjoy some quiet time and catch up on correspondence or work if needed.

THE
KIDS'
BEDROOM

Creating clever rooms for the pint-sized personalities in your life is no easy task. Ideally they'll be cool and funky (so the kids like them), good quality and affordable (so you like them), and somewhat cohesive with the style of decorating in the rest of the house. Whether you are decorating a nursery for a baby who is yet to arrive in the world, or working with your own little growing concern with ideas and insights about the design direction his or her room should take, I encourage you to channel your youthful spirit and create a room that is as fabulously one of a kind as your child.

PREPPY JUNIOR SUITE

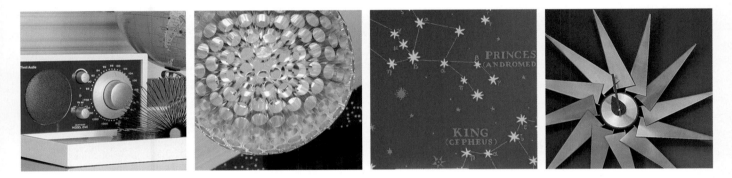

Designing a bedroom for a tween boy is no easy task. He isn't a little boy anymore, so cars, trucks, trains, planes, boats, robots, and superheroes are out of the question. When tasked with the challenge of dressing a blank-slate bedroom in a manner befitting a growing boy, I opted to look ahead a decade or so to his college days and embrace the influences of preppy patterns and varsity style to create a boys' club atmosphere that won't soon be deemed too juvenile.

SCOTTISH PRIDE ←

Fabrics that are well suited to a young man's room can be tricky to find. While he's obviously too old for theme-park caricatures, it can be tough to find something with colour and pattern that strikes the right chord, so that's why I'm drawn to tartan — it offers just the right blend of sophistication and boyish charm. With roots dating back to the 1700s, the classic Black Watch combination of blue, green, and black is an all-time favourite of mine. But with hundreds of patterns and colours to choose from, there's sure to be a tartan to fit your young man's colour preferences. Instead of searching in decorating shops for the best tartan interpretation, head straight to the garment-trade fabric stores to find the real deal. This woven wool offers quality and value in equal amounts.

GO WITH THE GROOVE ↘

Some might say that a stippled stucco ceiling resembles the surface of the moon and would be well suited to this night-sky-themed bedroom, but replacing the textured ceiling was a top priority for this space. To cut down on dust and add a varsity vibe to the sloped ceiling, I had 4-by-8-foot sheets of V-groove panelling attached to the ceiling and used flat-stock trim to cover the seams and frame the outer perimeter. The panelling proved to be a quick and easy way to transform the ceiling from its bland beginnings.

THE BED GOES BESPOKE ↕
Finding a bed that looks neither childish nor grown-up can be a challenge.
Since kids seem to collect a vast array of treasures and a never-ending
assortment of "stuff," you can never have too much storage to swallow
up their belongings and keep them organized. This bed started with
a pair of black-painted, freestanding bookshelves that I transformed into
a headboard wall by connecting the towers with an upper shelf and a piece
of V-groove panelling for an easy-to-achieve customized solution.

OVER THE MOON ↕
Once you've set sail on a course that embraces a night-sky motif,
I'm all in favour of keeping the theme on track with lighting that's got
a planetary vibe. Made from aluminum tubes, this moonlike orb pendant
adds a dappled effect to the star-covered walls and is sure to get a nod
of approval from even the most difficult-to-please tween client.

BREAK IT UP ↕

By installing a chair-rail profile about 3 feet off the floor, you can cut down on the expense of wallpaper by incorporating a lighter paint hue on the lower section of the wall to keep the room bright during daylight hours. To add extra impact, embrace your stars-and-stripes concept and add a playful touch to the paint scheme that channels collegiate charm by painting an accent band of bold colour just below the rail. Thanks to painter's tape, it's easy to get a crisp edge and a straight line.

UNDER THE STARS ↘

Wallpaper isn't just for pretty and proper rooms—it can be used in a lighthearted and fun way. Leave it to the master of varsity class and boyish charm, Ralph Lauren, to envision a night-sky-inspired wallpaper that's sure to charm your young astrologer with a map of the constellations that features glow-in-the-dark stars. Lights-out has never been better!

BUILT TO LAST ↕

Boys aren't known for being kind and gentle to their furnishings, so thankfully there are indestructible offerings that have proven their staying power over the decades, such as the American classic "tanker desk," which was a practical and indestructible staple in schools, offices, and governmental institutions from the mid-1940s to the 1970s. Pair your machine-age desk with a vintage banker's chair for another 1940s classic that provides durability and ergonomic comfort with staying-power style. These chairs are easy to find in vintage or consignment shops, likely due to their sturdy construction, and look great when sprayed a fun colour or left in their natural-oak finish.

BOHEMIAN BEDROOM

Infusing your home with a stylish motif or colour trend presents a challenge: How do you achieve a look that is relevant without regretting the makeover when the next great design direction is revealed? The trick is to experiment with colour and pattern in small doses and to embrace trend-focused elements in creative, low-investment ways. With a few easy tricks, you can change up your accents again when the next new hue or pattern catches your fancy.

PLAY IT SAFE ⇥

Experimenting with daring colours and trendy patterns can be intimidating, but it's possible to embrace a fashion-forward palette while still making a noncommittal colour infusion in an all-white and cream room by injecting jolts of high-voltage colour in accents that are easy to change. A patterned quilt, a few colourful pillows, artwork, and accessories will take any room from white to wow without a lifetime commitment. Making daring colour decisions should be an attainable and fun adventure, so shop wisely and savour the satisfaction of adding zing to your decor for a palatable price tag.

SKIP A CENTURY ⇕

I never cease to be amazed by the transformative power of a fresh coat
of paint. While treasure hunting for bargains, I found an Eastlake buffet and
occasional chair for impossible-to-resist prices. These Victorian-era elements
can read as too serious and mature for a kid's bedroom if left in their original
wood finish, but when sprayed in glossy white paint, the geometric profiles
and ornamental carving lend a whimsical mood to century-old finds.

MAP OUT AN ALTERNATIVE ↘

There are plenty of innovative ways to add colour, pattern, and interest to your walls if you look beyond the typical definition of "art." A large vintage pull-down map, hung with its original roller mechanism intact, reflects the room's vibrant colour scheme and provides a big-impact solution on a low-impact budget.

TABLE A MOTION ↕

Adding a desk area to a kid's bedroom doesn't need to occupy as much space as an executive suite. In many homes, computers are kept in the main area for adult supervision, so a smaller tabletop surface may suffice in place of a standard-issue desk. I added a painted wood tabletop to a trio of architectural salvage brackets that came painted in perky pink to offer a multipurpose area that can be used as a writing desk or a dressing table.

SHIFT YOUR FOCUS ↗

One of the best ways to make a statement with a saturated hue is to pick up a paintbrush. With a single quart of paint, you can quickly and inexpensively make a bold stroke on a small ceiling or section of wall and add an accent colour to any room. Instead of painting what lies right before your eyes, why not draw your gaze upwards and treat the ceiling to a bold new hue?

PATTERN PLAY

The arrival of a new baby signals a fresh start, and the opportunity to decorate with excitement and exuberance. But it's important to balance the needs of a tiny little human with thoughts of the future. I've always been a proponent of taking a long view towards nursery decor and trying to avoid the urge to festoon the room in cutesy, juvenile motifs and decorations that will soon tire and feel outdated for the room of a rapidly growing child. Instead of embracing all things adorable in nursery decor, I try to branch out and create a collection of fun yet flexible pieces that will stand the test of time.

LOOKING UP ✐

Making the most of every surface and every element of an existing space helps transform a room from a blank canvas into a fully realized vision. When thinking about how babies experience their rooms, I found myself occupied with thoughts of staring at the ceiling, which morphed into imagining how to apply the principle of "blue sky" thinking to this room. If you think of your ceiling as the fifth wall, it can become a feature instead of a nonstarter. Putting this strong paisley pattern on the walls might translate as busy and formal, but applying a traditional element in an unexpected way takes it in a fun, contemporary direction.

LOOK TO DAD'S CLOSET FOR INSPIRATION ⬆

I'm a tactile person and need to touch and feel anything that I'm considering using in every room. Your home isn't just filled with decorative objects that look good. Your nest should be feathered with elements that *feel* good, especially if they're coming in contact with newborn skin. Shirting cotton that is commonly used for men's dress shirts is some of the finest, smoothest fabric I've ever touched. It's also reasonably priced, so why not take Dad's shirt fabric and turn it into baby's bedding? You'll only need a few yards to create custom pillows, sheets, and duvet covers, and your baby will have the best nest to inspire deep sleep!

LINK THE EYE LINE ✐

If you're pondering pattern on the ceiling, be sure to create a visual connection that helps focus your sight line at eye level. By dressing the window in a strong blue-and-white geometric pattern, a seamless connection between the window and ceiling is created and pulls the focus down.

SAY IT WITH STRIPES ➻

While you may never embrace my idea of applying paisley punch to your ceiling, you might want to wake up your walls with sporty stripes. Start by extracting a collection of colours that appear in one of your key fabrics, then match them to paint chips and buy a quart of each. Use painter's masking tape to mark wide bands in varying widths along the length of the wall (don't make the stripes too narrow, as they will accentuate any unevenness in your taping job). Use a small roller or brush, and you'll have a dramatically dynamic wall of stripes in no time. Note: do try to enlist the help of a friend, as it's much easier to wrangle long lengths of tape if someone is on the opposite end to keep it stuck to the wall instead of you!

GET OVER THE GLIDER ↤

It seems that a glider or baby rocker is considered de rigueur on the baby inventory list. My predisposition is to react against anything that I'm told I must use, and I immediately want to find a better solution. The reality is that there will be late nights, early mornings, not enough sleep, and lots of nursing with a newborn. *But*, there's no rule that says you need to be chained to a decoratively uninspired piece of furniture during all these sleep-deprived days. Trust me on this one (I did the rocker for baby 1 and never used it for baby 2). If you can find a groovy chair that's easy to get in and out of (so you don't wake the dozing baby) with a high back (so you can rest your head), you're golden. During my quest for an alternative solution, I discovered one that rocks *and* swivels *and* is covered in punchy orange felt . . . sold!

DON'T BE TOO SERIOUS ↤

Even if you're trying to decorate for the long haul, remember that kids' rooms need to be fun and playful. Look for inexpensive fabrics and patterns to add a sense of whimsy. Oversized ball fringe cost less than $30 to buy and lends an unexpected twist to the modern graphic-print drapes. This may not be to everyone's taste, but it makes me smile every time I see it. I encourage you to find the elements and embellishments that make you smile when you walk into a room, and to embrace the fun side of design!

STIMULATE THE SENSES ↘

We're told that newborns only see black and white and that stimulating their brain development with bold patterns is important. You can make an artistic statement while embracing the early development of your baby by taking a trip to your local bookstore or stationery shop to find images to frame. How about a fabulous set of flash cards depicting all your favourite animals in bold black and white? At less than $3 apiece, I couldn't pass them up. They're easy to finish in custom or ready-made frames and add an immediate hit of bold contrast.

POTTY TALK ↘

Many elements of nursery decor are short-lived necessities as opposed to long-term staples. Take the changing table, for example; you'll only need this dedicated-usage piece of furniture for a couple of years. Instead of wasting dollars on what's destined to become obsolete in your home, I suggest selecting something that provides a more flexible solution. A solid-oak server from a consignment shop, resprayed in a shade of night sky, makes an ideal changing table (for now) and will be a useful piece elsewhere in the home later. Just be sure to check that the top of the piece of furniture will accommodate the size of a changing pad.

NEUTRAL NURSERY

Some expectant parents gravitate towards classic nursery themes and tried-and-true colour palettes when it comes time to prepare for the stork's delivery of a fresh little bundle of love. True-blue schemes accented with iconic boy-friendly motifs can create charming results, but some clients request a design direction that breaks away from the pack. For a design-enthused blogger with a desire for a one-of-a-kind nursery, I took the room on a wild adventure by introducing safari-inspired accents and a naturally neutral palette.

GO WILD ←

It's easy to add architectural interest to a small, boxy room with trim details. Crown moulding creates a defined transition between walls and ceiling (and invites the use of an accent colour on the ceiling), while a plate rail allows you to embrace different wall treatments above and below. Neutral grass cloth above the rail adds a warm tone and texture, while monochromatic zebra-print wallpaper jazzes up the lower section without being overpowering.

SEEK OUT THE UNEXPECTED ←

To find furnishings with character and personality that will stand the test of time and not appear too juvenile as your child grows, look beyond baby-specific furniture stores. Buying side tables, dressers, and footstools in vintage-furniture or consignment shops or at a flea market will allow you to stretch your budget while creating a one-of-a-kind environment filled with pieces that will grow with your child. A ready-made diaper-changing-pad topper can be bought with the crib and sprayed to match. If it rests on the dresser, it can be removed when no longer needed, but the dresser can remain an integral piece of the room for the long haul.

PRACTICE MATH ⭥
Cribs can be expensive. If you want to add some impact and excitement to yours,
buy a sturdy yet inexpensive one and have it painted the colour of your choice.
Bright green is energetic and impactful but can still be gender neutral
if you don't know the sex of the baby when you are decorating.

—

UNIFY YOUR FOUND TREASURES ⭥
The golden-oak finish of this library cabinet with glass doors was looking
tired, but painting the frame of the bookshelves to match the dresser and
accenting the shelves to match the side table and crib helps unify
all the furnishings for a cohesive statement. Glass doors make it
easy to see what's inside while keeping the contents dust free.

GET SOME RETAIL THERAPY ↕

Even an awkwardly laid-out closet can be made more efficient if you create effective storage by adding small shelves in hard-to-reach areas. By installing shelves at eye level and using baskets to help you stay organized by designating what goes where, a cramped closet won't be overcome with clutter. In many old houses, the closets aren't deep enough to accommodate the depth of a hanger from front to back, but if you visit a retail-display supply company, you can buy store hanging fixtures that allow you to put your hangers facing outwards.

BE ADVENTUROUS WITH ART ↕

Make your own art by painting leaves, placing them facedown on artist's paper, covering with a sheet of wax paper, and then creating an imprint by rolling the wax paper with a rolling pin. You'll have best results if you use leaves with a defined vein structure that aren't too thick. Simple shapes rendered in a single colour to connect with the room decor are an inexpensive way to dress bare walls.

PLAYFUL PARADISE

It's well-known that little girls love pink and princesses, and all things girlie and sparkly, but that doesn't mean every bedroom scheme needs to look as though it were inspired by cotton candy and executed in a way that is stiflingly sweet. Pink may be the most prevalent colour available in mass-market kids' decor, but it's not the only hue in the rainbow that can make a little girl happy. For a bedroom shared by a toddler and a baby, I stepped outside the pink zone to achieve a look that's playful and happy without being too predictable.

COLOUR ME ANYTHING

I often find the offering of available finishing options on basic products uninspiring and feel compelled to add my own twist in an effort to create a unique result. Bunk beds are a popular choice amongst little kids, since the idea of sleeping up high, climbing the ladder, and having not one but two beds are all exciting concepts to a small person. If the bunk bed you've decided to purchase isn't available in the colour of your choice, you can always paint it to make your little princess happy. After all, what little girl wouldn't prefer pale lavender over a plain white bed? If you plan to paint a new piece of furniture, it's best to paint all the individual elements separately for maximum coverage and then assemble it.

CLEAN UP WELL

You can never have too much storage in a kid's room, especially if a play area has been incorporated. The little ones may be small, but they tend to have lots of stuff, and every toy comes with plenty of pieces, so the key to keeping it tidy and maintaining a sense of order relies on whether it's easy for your kids to learn how to take part in the cleanup. If storage solutions are easy to access and designated for specific purposes, you may find that, at the end of each play session, it's easy to scoop up all the pieces and toss them back where they belong. A round storage ottoman with a removable top can even double as a play table, and the upholstered frame makes it a soft, multifunctional addition to the room.

MAKE IT EASY

Creating a unique kids' bedroom is a great choice. To help make the process as easy and cost-effective as possible, I recommend selecting a single colour to use as your main foundation for the room. Pulling together a mix-n-match scheme of fabrics is achievable if you are working in a monochromatic palette, but it's more challenging to find multiple options with a coordinated palette in a multicolour scheme. You can always inject a secondary colour through solid fabrics, decorative accents, or paint finishes. Mixing a polka-dot, a stripe, and a mini print with the scenic wallpaper created a textured mix of patterns for a lighthearted, kid-friendly concept, and the hints of lilac make it a fashion-forward combination that's a refreshing departure from bubble-gum pink.

ENCOURAGE SWEET DREAMS

Children's books are intended to delight and stimulate the imagination with their charming illustrations. You can bring the story to life by wrapping the walls in a wallpaper pattern that makes it feel as though your little one is sleeping amidst the pages of an adventure story. The whimsical drawings on this design are playful without being juvenile, so the pattern should be an appealing choice for years to come.

FRESH & FUN BEDROOMS

What could be more fun than decorating a pair of bedrooms for three bubbly little bundles of fun? Not much, in my book! Harnessing the joy, happiness, and unbridled energy of little kids and transforming it into rooms that embrace their lively spirit is always an adventure. When you strip away the grown-up need for poise and polish, the decorating direction takes on a purely lighthearted spirit, fuelled by the desire to create a cozy, happy nest that stimulates the imagination and celebrates the freedom of being a child.

DON'T WASTE YOUR LEFTOVERS ←
After selecting a swirling paisley print for the windows, I added a whimsical polka-dot band along the leading edge for a bit of pattern play. When left with an extra scrap of fabric, I sewed it into a changing-pad cover that's easy to remove and wash. Once you've recovered a chair, sewn drapes, and selected the fabrics, you'll likely have some pieces left over, which can be used to make cheery and colourful accents. Try attaching iron-on inter-facing to some of the scraps and cutting them into triangles with pinking shears, then attaching them to a long piece of ribbon to create a pennant on the wall.

BREAK AWAY FROM THE PACK ←
I love thinking out of the box when it comes to colour and fabric choices. To create a kid-friendly space that complemented yet departed from the adjacent siblings' room in cool watery hues, I relied on a warm and spicy mix to perk up this pint-sized nursery.

TEA TIMES TWO ↕
Tea towels aren't just for cleanup. After discovering adorable embroidered kitchen linens, I sewed the towels together and added ribbon loops at the edges to create a handy wall-hung laundry bag (since anyone who's ever changed a diaper knows all too well how fast laundry accumulates with a little one). For an extra accent of this adorable pattern, I also created a little lumbar cushion for the armchair simply by using the decoratively embroidered half of the towel to ensure Mama would be sitting pretty during snuggles and feeding.

PLAN AHEAD ↕
During the early days of infancy when babies are tiny, little immobile bundles, their needs seem so simple. Before you know it, that little bundle will be walking, talking, and growing faster than you ever imagined. Instead of buying baby-specific furnishings, I'm a firm believer in looking farther afield to find the right long-term furnishings. An extra-wide French Provincial bureau offers enough counter area to accommodate a changing pad and baby supplies for the early days, and plenty of storage drawers to hold a growing girl's wardrobe in the years to come.

GO CUSTOM ON A DIY BUDGET

Small, shared rooms can be tricky to furnish, since every inch counts, and so does every dollar! While the vertical efficiency of bunk beds is appealing, I find the extra height can dominate the room and overpower the space in some scenarios. I devised an alternate built-in bed that would accommodate two kids on one even plane while giving each their own space to cozy up. Have no fear; you can still execute a successful DIY project without a full set of power tools. If you measure thrice (twice is never enough) and plan out your installation, you can have your materials precut at your local big-box store, then simply install them at home with a drill (it also helps to have a saw in case your measurements need a bit of adjusting).

BED-BUILDING BASICS

I used shelves on edge as the supports for the underside of the bed (at 12-by-36 inches, there was no trimming needed), then had two slabs of plywood cut to fit the standard size of a twin mattress, attached 2-by-4-inch boards to the outside wall to support the bed platform, and dressed the cut edge of the plywood and shelves with preprimed window-casing profiles. For $200 in supplies, I was able to create one cool bed to fit two cool kids.

GET ONLINE FOR INNOVATIVE ART

Forget pounding the pavement in search of the right art to dress up your little one's room, and let your fingers do the walking as you shop online. I discovered animal art decals made from vintage wallpaper that make a big impact while eliminating the need to invest additional dollars in framing. These exotic critters simply require a bit of wallpaper paste (included with purchase) to affix them to the wall. From elephant to giraffe, lion to alligator, there's an animal to appeal to your little tiger!

THE
BATHROOM

Bathrooms are right up at the top of the list with kitchens as the best rooms in the house to renovate for maximum resale value. The renovation of an existing bath, or the creation of one within a new house, offers an opportunity to carve out a little space designated for pampering, primping, and rejuvenation. In an ideal world, your bathroom should be akin to your own private spa, but in reality it's probably more like a turnstile during the morning rush hour. If the start of your day is frenetic, it's my hope that your evening ritual offers more time to enjoy the finer details of bath design. When the house is quiet and everyone has stopped scurrying around, you'll be able to savour the return on your investment.

BLUSH BATHROOM

Don't we all dream of having a beautiful bathroom at home that combines luxury, sophistication, glamour, and practicality? At some point, every bathroom needs a refresh. But often a simple refresh isn't possible, and a total rethink is what's ultimately needed to transition from drab to dramatic. Taking inspiration from the rich character and ornate detail in Victorian homes, the design of this bathroom marries the simplicity and style of a classically timeless black-and-white palette with an accent of saturated colour.

RETHINK YOUR SPACE ↥

If a "back to the studs" gut job is on the agenda and you've got a roomy bathroom space to work with, why not play around with the layout and see if you can dream up a better overall plan for what goes where? You may not be able to alter certain fixed elements, but part of the excitement of renovating is redefining how to make the room work best for your lifestyle.

PROBLEM SOLVING ↣

The key to any successful renovation project is making the most of the challenges you encounter. To move the vanity beside the window, the wall needed to be built out about 5 inches to conceal the pipes. Instead of building out the entire wall, I designed a built-in backsplash and ledge to offer a pretty place to keep bathroom necessities close at hand (and out of the way) while solving a practical issue.

THINK PINK ↰

The general rule with renovations is to play it safe when it comes to matters of palette and pattern. If you're worried about resale value or unsure whether a current trend will be the right choice for the long term, it's best to stick to timeless and basic materials for all of the elements that are tough to change (such as tile and counters). But this doesn't mean you can't have oodles of fun and indulge in a fashion-forward accent hue. By limiting your use of colour to elements that are easy to change (such as accessories, drapes, paint, and even a small accent chair), you'll always be able to add an au courant accent to your monochromatic masterpiece.

HAVING IT ALL ↕

Sometimes you need to make trade-offs to get everything you want. If a custom-built vanity isn't in your price bracket, consider ordering a ready-made vanity base with "his and her" sinks and buy an inexpensive antique or vintage cabinet to store all your towels and necessities. The polished-chrome exposed legs on this vanity are a sculptural and shiny throwback to the style of bathrooms from days gone by, as well as a more sophisticated design statement than your standard vanity design.

SHOWCASE YOUR FITTINGS ↰

If you're looking to create a master bath complete with authentic style and attention to detail, consider a shower system with exposed fittings. Instead of running the pipes that connect the valve to the showerhead behind the wall, this stylish system simply connects to hot and cold water rough-ins to add a decorative wow factor and old-school glam to your shower stall.

SOOTHING RETREAT

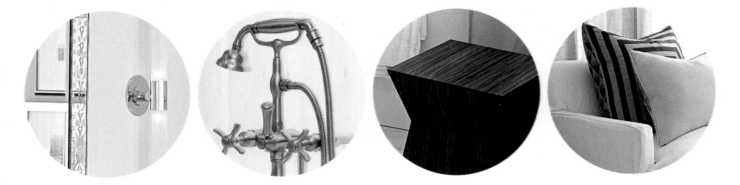

When the opportunity presents itself to take a diamond in the rough and polish it into a gem of a family home, an exciting renovation adventure unfolds. For a professional couple with an appetite for modern design and a love of historical charm, the vision was to create a bathroom escape within a Victorian home. To maximize the available space, a former sunporch was reconfigured to create a luxe and airy oasis for pampering.

MASTER THE MIX ←
Add a hint of traditional elegance to a vanity with contemporary lines by using book-matched decorative veneer on the door and drawer faces. The pattern in this crotch-mahogany veneer mimics ripples on water and elevates the vanity from simple bath station to fine furniture. It's the perfect blend for a modern bathroom in a century home.

IGNORE CONVENTION ←
Instead of using wall sconces as decorative bathroom fixtures, I like to install pendants. This lighting alternative allows you to mount a mirror that runs the full width of the vanity and accentuates the ceiling height by emphasizing the vertical line of the hanging fixture. If you select a pendant with a glass shade, you'll have plenty of light to illuminate your face and ensure you always look your best.

BE COMPLEMENTARY ←
Tie in a reference to your vanity by ordering a custom-sized mirror made with a stock profile or picture frame in the same wood tone as your vanity. The two pieces will look as if they were made for each other.

LIGHTEN UP ←

By nature, bathrooms are filled with hard, durable surfaces, such as stone, glass, and metal, and can benefit from a lighter touch through an infusion of more delicate materials. Drapes made from handkerchief linen are an alternative to typical window-covering solutions such as shutters and blinds and offer a lightweight (and inexpensive) option. When used unlined, handkerchief linen can easily be washed, and the thin weight of the fabric allows the light to filter in while still offering complete privacy.

MAKE IT WHITE ↕

When considering an upholstered piece of furniture for a spacious en suite bathroom, choose a covering that is washable and durable. Soft, prewashed white twill continues the theme of crisp and fresh finishes

and is easy to keep looking bright and white since it's a removable slipcover. Lounging and luxuriating in your bathrobe is looking like a reality with this addition.

LAYER IT ↕

You don't need glitz and glam to attain luxury. Sometimes it's not the material but how you use it that generates the best results. Instead of focusing on what's fancy and special, mixing various sizes of similar materials is an easy way to create simple elegance. For a shower stall, try alternating between large-format marble tiles and bands of smaller brick-pattern mosaic ones. The bricks create subtle horizontal stripes, while the grey and white veining in the large tiles reinforces the palette of the drapes, walls, and furnishings.

SPARKLY TEEN SUITE

Worrying about making your renovations seem timeless and enduring shouldn't prevent you from expressing a sense of fun and experimenting with your love of colour. It may be unwise to install bold colour in materials that are difficult to change, such as tile and counters, but you can still add lots of cheery accents to the room. Any tile scheme can benefit from an injection of cheery colour with towels and storage baskets in the trendy hue of your choice. Using low-investment accessories and accents means you can feel good about sprucing up your colour scheme in a new palette whenever the next wave of trends rolls in.

BE AN ORIGINAL ➳

Once you know what size vanity will fit in your bathroom, you've got the opportunity to create a one-of-a-kind showpiece that will cost you less than a custom-made option if you shop wisely. This vintage hall table turned vanity came with a pair of drawers and intricate brass hardware that upped the ante in decorative details. A carpenter added the shelf to provide a spot to stack towels and baskets, while the curvaceous details add a feminine touch that sets the tone for a girlie glam bathroom.

KEEP IT ON TOP ➳

An undercounter or drop-in bathroom sink will offer a uniform height across the counter surface, but if you are converting a piece of furniture into a vanity, you might want to consider a vessel sink for its space-saving features. Instead of being cut into the drawers below, the sink simply sits on top of the counter. You'll need to create a channel to accommodate the drain, but the drawers can still be useful if your carpenter notches out the necessary clearance for the plumbing.

TAKE IT HIGHER ➶

A standard backsplash ranges in height from 4 to 6 inches, but you can make yours whatever height you choose. When using a vessel sink, adding some extra height to the backsplash will keep your walls safe from water. To accentuate the extra height and reference the sculptural details of the base unit, add a scalloped detail to the corners. It won't cost much, and every pretty little detail counts in the final result.

STEP IT UP ➶

Even the simplest tiles can benefit from a little attention to detail with the layout. Combining cream and white ceramic tiles in a herringbone pattern takes a simple staple material and turns it into a graphic and geometric statement. Combining the warmth of cream with pure white results in a bath that reads as bright and light without being too stark.

GO BACK IN TIME ↕

Add a sweet finishing touch to your counter surface with vintage accessories that are both functional and frilly. These hobnail milk-glass collectibles can be found inexpensively at flea markets and consignment shops, and the polka-dot pattern adds a youthful and fun infusion.

SUBURBAN SPA

You may not be able to schedule (or afford) a regular spa getaway in your frantic everyday life, yet the restorative, relaxing, and rejuvenating elements we automatically associate with the pampering rituals of a luxury spa remain a constant source of inspiration in bathroom design. When it came time to envision a large master en suite bath in a subdivision home, I relied on my trademark wispy and watery palette to create a serene and subtly hued, spa-fresh *salle de bains*.

MAKE NO MISTAKE ⇥

Kitchens and baths are costly to renovate (or build), so I would encourage you to focus your spending on neutral material choices that will stand the test of time, both in terms of durability and style. There's no reason you should live without colour in your bath (if you so desire), but when you've got resale thoughts on your mind, I suggest you temper your daring inner design diva with a dose of understated restraint.

SOAK FREELY ⇥

It's no secret that I gravitate to a freestanding bath over a built-in model. The sculptural element of an oval tub introduces a break from all the boxy forms of the vanity and shower stall. By floating your bath in an area with breathing room, you'll have flexibility to introduce elements of softness, such as drapes that float behind the bath. Opt for a washable, breezy fabric, such as eyelet, and leave drapes unlined for easy fluff and fold care.

BREAK OUT OF THE MOULD ⇥

While the common shape for a bathroom vanity mirror is round or rectilinear, you can customize your reflection in an unusual shape. Made from standard picture-framing profiles, the tall and narrow proportions of his and hers mirrors in this bathroom accentuate the ceiling height while also allowing enough wall space to install artwork as well as high-impact elegance in the form of double-arm, crystal wall sconces.

PLAY WITH PROPORTION ⇠

After selecting your main floor material, there's no need to limit yourself to a single size or shape of tile (or stone). In the same way that you'd combine a few different fabrics for upholstered furnishings, you can mix and match a number of different tiles to bring a more dynamic and textured look to your tile story. It doesn't cost much to define a large tiled area with a few bands of smaller mosaic to create the effect of a carpet detail underfoot, yet it definitely breaks up the monotony of using a single size of stone throughout.

MAKE IT SPARKLE ✓

I'm always thinking about ways to dress up average elements to create innovative results. If your budget only allows for a standard Shaker door profile, consider adding a custom touch and hint of glamour, if you desire. The linear profile of a Shaker door allows for

an easy aftermarket retrofit of mirrored panels. I used antiqued mirrors, which I ordered with a predrilled hole in the centre of each panel to accommodate the addition of pressed-glass knobs that sparkle and shimmer as they float against the reflective backdrop.

GET LEGGY ⫶

Once you've designed your vanity to accommodate all the storage you need and all the counter space you crave, elevate the hulking mass of your double-sink creation by incorporating furniture details. This Queen Anne–style leg references a traditional furniture detail and brings a fluid finishing touch to a simple vanity. You'll never regret breaking away from the pack and doing something different to make your renovation a unique statement of personal style.

MINIMALIST EN SUITE

Carving out a house that fits your family's style can be a liberating experience if your home offers options to shuffle the allocation of space and redefine the overall program of the house. An addition on the back of a grand Edwardian home freed up former bedroom space to become an airy en suite bath with minimalist influences for a couple of urban professionals with a growing young family.

KEEP IT SIMPLE ⇥

When designing a contemporary bathroom, keeping a focus on unadorned details is best. After opting to emphasize natural-wood finishes, the pattern in the grain of a walnut vanity takes centre stage as the most commanding visual feature. With full overlay drawers and integrated handles, the vanity is pared down to the simplest possible profile. Instead of a counter with a carved swan or ogee profile, select a clean, square edge that allows the veining and tonal variation on your countertop to be the main attraction.

KNOW WHERE IT ENDS ⇥

The toughest aspect of successful renovations is making sure you are prepared for every detail in bringing all the components together for a fabulous finished product. It may seem that small details such as trim and finishing touches can be figured out later, but it's best to map it all out in advance. Tall, traditional baseboards are a consistent finish throughout this house, and the simple wall-to-wall vanity sits right at the top. Planning ensures that all the pieces of your puzzle fit together perfectly during the final stages.

AMP UP YOUR NEUTRALS ↩

The common perception is that the neutral palette is limited to the tonal range of all things muddy in colour, from beige to brown, with a bit of grey thrown in for good measure. I actually take a broader view of neutral and extend my definition to include anything within the natural spectrum. Silvery ocean blues and soft grassy greens make all those muddy shades so much more dynamic with a subtle accent. Without seeming the least bit "colourful," a healthy dose of watery grey-blue was added to this understated palette as the backdrop to the shower and vanity, and in the softer finishing touches of drapes and towels.

HIDE THE EVIDENCE ↗

If you are trying to create a seamless transition between the bathroom and the shower without a curb to delineate the boundary between wet and dry zones, moving the drain from the centre of the stall is the way to go. Thanks to trough drains,

you can relocate your shower drain to run the full width along one side of your shower stall. With a shallow slope to one side, you'll be able to use any nonslip material in the size and pattern of your choice without chopping it into little pieces, thereby making the drain a disappearing act.

MANAGE YOUR EXPOSURE ↩

Having large windows in your bathroom doesn't necessitate exposing yourself to the neighbours or keeping the drapes closed to shut out the light. When replacing windows during a renovation, you can order the panes of glass to be made from sandblasted or acid-etched glass instead of clear, so you'll always have privacy, and light too! This mixing of traditional details and contemporary finishes is a consistent approach throughout the entire home — one that celebrates the best of all things old and new.

QUAINT COUNTRY CHARMER

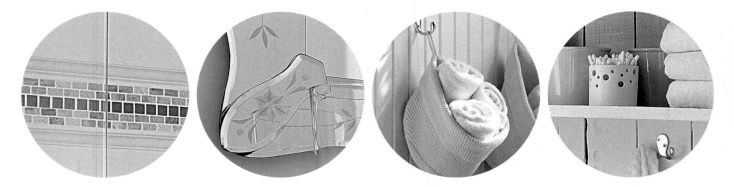

A limited budget shouldn't deter you from making a marked improvement in your bathroom. Without custom orders and long lead times, it is possible to update your bathroom on a budget that's easy to embrace. Keeping all of the plumbing fixtures in their existing locations and focusing on giving the room a stylish retrofit will afford you a sweet home spa. I took on the challenge of revamping this bath with flea-market finds and basic in-stock materials to show that it's possible to achieve a stylish result on a shoestring budget and a short timeline.

GET CHARM FOR LESS CASH ↠
When you are on a budget, you won't likely have the funds to tile all around the bathroom, but you still need a barrier against water splashing from the bathtub. V-groove wood panelling is relatively inexpensive to buy and easy to install. If you are looking for the most economical solution, you can buy it in sheet format instead of individual board lengths and determine an overall finished height that allows you to maximize every sheet to get two panels. Once it's installed and dressed with a chair rail and baseboard as a finishing touch, prime and paint the panelling with a glossy trim paint for a solution that's durable, scrubbable, and charming too!

MAKE ORDER A TEAM EFFORT ↠
A row of hooks placed about 40 inches off the ground guarantees that there's a spot for everyone's towel, and room to keep a few extras close at hand. Easy and inexpensive to install, these hardware-store basic hooks help even little kids do their part to keep everything neat and tidy in a shared family bath.

SCORE A SAVVY SOAKER ↠
While a new soaker tub might break the bank for your reno budget, fabulous vintage options are available. You should be able to source one online for a fraction of the price of any new freestanding tub. A classic claw-foot bathtub is easy to install and adds instant old-school charm for a pretty look with old-world appeal.

TUCK IT AWAY ↘

Every bathroom can benefit from plenty of storage for toiletries and products, but you may not be able to find the look you want for the price you can afford. A small vintage cabinet, bought for a steal at a yard sale, can be transformed with a fresh coat of paint and topped with a drop-in sink that's cut into the existing top of the cabinet. A standard vanity ranges from 20 to 22 inches in depth, so just make sure you choose a cabinet with enough depth to accommodate your sink.

REPEAT THE PATTERN ←

If you are only tiling select areas in your bathroom, you might as well make them as pretty as possible. To dress up a simple white shower stall, a few accent bands were added at eye level. To reinforce the two-tone combination of the band, the same materials were installed on the floor, except in a larger-format mosaic. Honed green slate and watery Ming Green marble add a special touch to an otherwise frugal tile scheme.

TURN IT UPSIDE DOWN ←

A ceramic tile chair-rail profile is intended to be installed with the thicker side at the top and the thinner profile at the bottom. If you are trying to combine standard-thickness ceramic tile with stone mosaic details, you will likely find that the mosaic pieces are thicker and protrude beyond the narrow portion of the chair-rail piece. The easy work-around is to invert the chair rail so the thicker edge buts up against the mosaic and the thin portion tapers down to meet the ceramic tile. By doing this, you'll have a crisp tile edge, and no one will be the wiser.

TREETOP ESCAPE

In some cases, renovation projects are straightforward and simple, with minor changes yielding major improvements. And then there are the jobs that are like a challenging puzzle. You'd never know from looking at the photos that this spacious bathroom started out as a tiny study on an upper floor of a landmark building with strict preservation guidelines that made the mandate of installing a luxurious master bath anything but easy to accomplish.

ROUND OFF ↦

When the goal of your bathroom design includes evoking a relaxing and pampering ambiance, focus on incorporating elegant touches that take it from basic to beautiful. A rounded silhouette on the vanity adds a more graceful line than the more common rectangular profile, yet still offers plenty of storage behind the burled-walnut cabinet doors. If you plan the interiors of your vanity carefully, you'll be able to add drawers beneath the sink, making it more efficient for storage. Continue the theme of curved edges with an oval mirror and orb-shaped apothecary jars for a bathroom that's sure to take the edge off.

HAVE IT ALL ↥

For a traditional bathroom with all the modern conveniences on your wish list, get creative with all available space. The angled bulkhead from a staircase in this bathroom proved to be the ideal location for mounting a sleek TV screen above an antique table that holds towels. Tub time just got a whole lot more entertaining!

MONOCHROMATIC MOSAIC

In any renovation there comes a point where the energy and enthusiasm starts to wane. When my clients ran out of steam, they simply closed the door and left a shell of a bathroom to be completed when they felt re-invigorated. Fast forward a couple of years, and I was called on to design a crisp minimal bathroom with streamlined simplicity and modern details.

PICK SIDES ←←

Typically tub fixtures are installed at the end of the bathtub opposite the slope for the backrest. But with a wide soaker tub, you may want to maintain the flexibility of using both ends of the tub, while also making it easier to control the flow of water without reaching across, so consider stacking your faucet and hand shower in a line on the front side of the bathtub and enjoy soaking in a nice hot bath from whatever end you choose.

FLOAT THE IDEA ←

Even a large, long vanity stained in a rich, dark wood tone needn't look like a giant mass glued to the floor. The lower section of any vanity doesn't offer much in terms of usable storage, so you might want to consider the visual benefits of a wall-hung, floating version. To keep the intersection between vanity and bathtub feeling open and airy, a cantilevered makeup table with concealed drawer was installed just below the height of the marble vanity counter to provide a perfect perch for applying makeup while being bathed in natural light from the adjacent window.

BUILD TO SUIT ↕

There are myriad options to enlarge your storage capabilities in any room. You can buy a piece of furniture, build a closet using studs and drywall, or you can create built-ins as a sleek furniture solution. A made-to-measure cabinet will save you

valuable inches on the thickness of drywall and framing and let you designate the exact combination of open and closed storage to meet your needs. With a sleek mitred frame, this spacious storage cabinet ensures that the calm order of this bath will never be overtaken by clutter.

LET IT FLOW ↕

If your goal is to experience Zen-like tranquillity within a modern envelope of space, your selection of materials will play a starring role in the result. With the mandate of making the room feel un-cluttered and slick, materials were selected to act as art, and the back wall connecting the bathtub and the shower was tiled from floor to ceiling in a Mondrian-esque mosaic of various-sized squares of marble in muted shades of grey.

COMPACT OASIS

When it comes to well-appointed bathrooms, it's not how much space you have that counts but how you make the most of it. For a pint-sized guest bath, the priority was to reference the owner's Gustavian heritage and dress the room in icy shades of mint and silver. Sparkly accents and cool metal finishes ensure that even the smallest space feels open and airy.

PLAY UP YOUR BEST FEATURES ↑
You can install tile only where you need it to protect against water spray, or you can accentuate the natural beauty of your chosen tile by covering an entire wall in wow-factor marble mosaic. More durable than wallpaper and way more exciting to look at than plain old paint, this treatment of a tiny space is equal measures practical and pretty.

SLICE IT UP ↦
Every detail matters and allows you to add layers of texture to your bathroom, so don't pass up on an element you desire if it doesn't fit the norm in terms of size. After stumbling upon delicate Venetian mirror sconces with glass arms, I simply could not pass them up. Without enough space for the sconces and a

standard-sized vanity mirror, I ordered up a narrow column of mirror edged at the top and bottom in a picture-frame profile that offers all the reflection needed for grooming.

GO BACK IN TIME ↑
Renovating a century-old residence with the goal of preserving character and traditional style can easily be accomplished thanks to reproduction plumbing fixtures and reclaimed building materials. Reconditioned door hardware will likely cost you less to buy at an architectural supply company than similar-quality new passage sets, and new plumbing fixtures with old-school white porcelain handle accents have classic charm and bring a nostalgic element to your newly renovated bath.

GEORGIAN REVIVAL

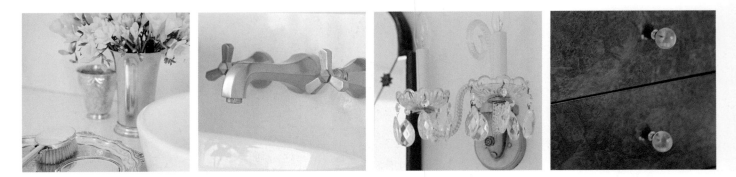

Arriving at the optimal configuration for a bathroom layout can feel like an insurmountable challenge when the space is limited and the wish list is long. Instead of admitting defeat and assuming the bathroom of your dreams was never meant to be, I suggest you get out your sketch pad and be prepared to exhaust every option before you concede. As part of a top-to-bottom gut job of a Georgian Revival town house, I was tasked with shoehorning an en suite bath into a compact floor plan, complete with all the amenities one would expect to find in an elegant upscale environment.

REINVENT TRADITION ➤

I am constantly inspired by the character and charm of old houses and thrive on finding new ways to work classic influences into modern homes by combining one part traditional luxe with one part contemporary chic. The profile for the vanity was borrowed from an antique breakfront, where the centre section projects beyond the ends that flank it. Burled-walnut-veneer doors give a nod to fine cabinetry, while a crisp frame delineates the vanity in a contemporary manner. The recessed side sections allow the cabinetry to be a safe distance from the swing of the shower door and the inevitable occasional overspray.

ADD A LITTLE POLISH ➤

When it comes to making a newly renovated bathroom fit into a century-old home, little touches go a long way. When working with exotic stones and decorative veneers, settling for standard-issue wall sconces just won't do. Vintage crystal double-arm wall sconces befitting a decadent dining room and delicate glass cabinetry knobs add a touch of sparkle to the mix, while vintage silver dresser accessories infuse the bathroom with old-world polish.

EXPLORE YOUR OPTIONS ←

We're all familiar with the larger-scale options for soaker tubs. If you don't have space for a small lap pool in your bathroom, never fear. The standard-issue soakers have generous proportions, but some manufacturers specialize in models with sleek and streamlined proportions. The advantage of this freestanding tub (which measures a mere 26 inches at its widest point) is that it trades width for height, resulting in a tub that fits in a narrow room and still lets you soak in bubbles up to your chin.

INDULGE YOUR EXTRAVAGANCE ←

A small bathroom requires less of everything when it comes to materials, which is a perfect rationale for indulging in better materials on every surface. You might consider slabs of onyx too decadent for your budget, but introducing it in a mosaic format is far less cost prohibitive. When it comes to integrating

mosaics, you'll find that most stone varieties are offered in a number of different shapes and patterns that allow you to achieve the best results. Two varieties of onyx and Thassos marble mosaics were used on the shower floor and wall, while a third configuration was mixed in with one-foot-square pieces of marble on the main floor to create a latticework. Intricate patterns and exotic materials are the magic mix in this bathroom.

KEEP IT CLEAR ↕

Installing your faucet as a wall mount will enable you to take full advantage of the available counter space in a compact layout. Moving the faucet into the wall allows you to push the sink back, which may prove helpful if you need to install a shallower-than-normal vanity to make the most of every inch when grappling with a narrow room and a robust wish list.

MIDTOWN MODERN

Since bathroom renovations inevitably gobble up the budget and make your savings account a thing of the past, it's important to have the details right, and to save money wherever possible. I've yet to encounter a project in my life where money is truly "no object," so my approach is always to get the most for the least and to make it look as though you sacrificed nothing to achieve your dream room. In reality, you have to keep your eye on the bottom line every step of the way to avoid drowning in debt when it's done. This bathroom served as a kitchen in a multiplex until I scrubbed it clean and created a home spa.

TUB TIME

Whether you install a freestanding bathtub or a built-in model is a matter of personal preference, but your choice can also impact your budget and time line. A freestanding option is ready to go and easy to install. Once the lines are roughed in, all you need is a visit from the plumber and you'll be ready to get out the rubber ducky. Meanwhile, the built-in option is more complex. The choreography goes something like this: carpenter builds the base, tiler covers the skirt, marble company measures for a stone surround (and you pay for the giant piece of marble that gets cut out of the middle), stone takes two weeks to arrive, then the plumber returns to hook it up, and you realize that the big built-in cost as much, or more, than that sleek stand-alone tub you thought was out of your budget!

MONEY MATTERS

It's only natural to be dazzled by the wide variety of mosaics designed to tempt your pocketbook. Generally priced around $15 per square foot (before installation charges), those pretty pieces can drive the overall cost of your reno way up. A typical 5-by-3-foot walk-in shower needs approximately 100 square feet of wall tile. If you do the math, you'll soon understand why wherever possible I use inexpensive white wall tile that costs about $2 or $3 a square foot, then dress it up with accent bands or a single accent wall using the fun stuff.

UP, DOWN, AND OVER ↣

Storage is a key consideration when I'm designing a vanity. Ensuring there's ample space to absorb all the products and tools we use to get ourselves ready to face the day is important. To break up the lines of a long vanity, I divided it into sections by function and varied the heights and depths of the units accordingly. The main section has cubbies for fresh towels, as well as the usual undersink storage; a small, lower makeup table has a concealed drawer and a kneehole to tuck away a stool; and a raised, six-drawer tower is both higher and deeper than the flanking units to create a furniture-inspired storage cabinet with room for everything you might ever need. Before you order a run-of-the-mill vanity, consider what the ideal scenario might look like for you!

YOURS, MINE, OR OURS ↣

A double vanity with two sinks is the norm in master bathroom layouts, but it's not a necessity. If you and your partner have the exact same schedule and tend to be in the bathroom at the same time during the morning rush, you will likely want to invest in two sinks. If you have a staggered schedule and aren't tripping over each other, it may not be necessary, so consider your schedules and your lifestyle before you double up.

AVIAN POWDER ROOM

Your powder room likely takes up the least amount of real estate in your entire home, but that's no reason to give it a pass in the style department. On the contrary, I think the powder room is an ideal place to experiment, have fun, and strike out in a slightly bolder direction than you might try in other areas. Since it's likely that you'll also spend the least amount of time in this room, you need not worry about creating a calming or soothing environment. Whatever your style statement, make it exciting and adventurous, and create a tiny room that offers a vibrant surprise every time you open the door!

GO OUT ON A LIMB ➙

A powder room is a stand-alone element that doesn't need to connect directly with the adjoining rooms, so don't be afraid to be bold and daring and try a colour or pattern you might not use in any other room. Or, for that matter, a combination of colours. With hints of ochre, orange, brown, and blue, the wallpaper in this powder room embraces many hues.

ACCENT TO CONNECT ➙

Using the whimsical bird-print wallpaper as the guiding design direction for the room, I extracted the ochre accent tone and repeated it on the drapes. Since the room has a lighthearted and playful mood, a simple cotton print makes the best companion, especially since it evokes the pattern of feathers. To add some panache to a monochromatic cotton print, consider sewing a length of grosgrain ribbon along the leading edge of the drapes in an accent colour.

PUT IT ON A PEDESTAL ➙

If you're tight on dollars, why not opt for a stunningly simple and classically elegant pedestal sink instead of a lacklustre and common vanity? Dress it up with an elegant faucet, and your powder room will have timeless appeal. The powder room doesn't generally require abundant storage, so it's a great place to save on the budget and buy an inexpensive pedestal. After all, you'll likely need to spend those savings on some dynamite wallpaper!

ADD A PERCH ↤

Think about your guests when outfitting the powder room and add a shelf or table (or both, if space permits) so they can rest a purse while powdering their nose. This petite Egyptian latticework shelf with drawer serves as both a functional and a decorative accent to the room.

SUMPTUOUS SOAKER

When designing bathrooms, I often think of classic European hotels and their inherent feeling of grandeur. That old-world, hotel-inspired look became my goal for this bathroom. Since this bath is located in a newer-build city home lacking in architectural features or historical details, I relied on antique elements and luxurious materials to bestow a look of traditional design and effortless elegance to a once soulless space.

SAY YES TO WALLPAPER ↕
In a well-proportioned bathroom with a good ventilation system and an enclosed shower, there's no reason not to use it. Wallpaper enlivens walls with pattern and texture. The neutral colour creates a soft backdrop while the raised texture of the hand-blocked pattern gives the illusion that the wallpaper might actually be hand-painted details on the wall.

BUY SOME HISTORY ↣
When trying to make a new space look old, it's imperative to use true vintage items. This reclaimed leaded-glass window came from a salvage store and was installed to let natural light flow into the master bathroom while still providing privacy. The combination of the window, antique chandelier, vintage chair, antique architectural prints, and antique bar cart add authentic charm that could not have been achieved with reproductions.

SLIP IN ↣
When deciding on the silhouette of your freestanding bathtub, consider a double-ended slipper tub. It's a true soaking tub with high sides so you can get up to your neck in bubbles, yet the narrow proportions don't sacrifice floor space, even allowing room for a chair. When the freestanding faucet is centred in the middle, both ends of the tub boast a spot to soak.

CROWNING GLORY ↣
Plaster crown moulding is the finishing touch for this well-appointed bathroom. While wood moulding seems like an easier and more readily available solution, it can shrink and crack if the humidity changes once it's installed. Wood options also need to be filled, primed, and then painted. Once plaster moulding is installed, it's ready to go. Combined with high baseboards, the plaster evokes that much-desired historical authenticity. To reinforce your colour scheme and highlight your lovely moulding, draw the lightest accent colour from your wallpaper and apply it to the ceiling.

THE FRAME-UP ⭥

Rather than thinking of the shower as a basic box and slapping up the ubiquitous 12-by-12-inch tiles in a standard grid pattern, I like to dress it up with details. You can achieve a panelled look by combining a 6-by-12-inch band of marble tiles as an outer perimeter, then use a band of chair-rail combined with rows of tiny mosaic tiles, then fill the remaining ground with your large-format tiles. Even when executed in a singular material such as this Bianco Perlino, the subtle pattern and varying sizes lend an elegant look to your shower.

MIRROR, MIRROR ↤

The relationship amongst your vanity, sink, mirror, and lighting needs to be considered as a total package. With a single sink, you can bring the sconces in from the sides of the vanity so the light lands where you need it most. This off-the-rack mirror with a cushion-cut frame is a step above the standard bathroom mirror, and the gilded frame references the rich, warm-metal accents used throughout the bathroom.

GO BEYOND THE BATH ⭥

Thanks to talented artisans and craftsmen, anything you imagine can be made to your exacting specifications. However, exquisite construction and attention to detail come with a commensurate price tag. When you're dreaming of intricate details, it's likely more cost effective to look for an antique or vintage serving piece for a dining room that can be repurposed. This vanity was converted from a 1950s-era buffet. The two centre doors hide the plumbing fixtures, while the side drawers and cupboards offer storage space. But it's the little details such as ormolu accents, delicate hardware, and the richness of the two-tone wood that make it a home run.

JUST A HALF WILL DO ↤

A half wall, commonly referred to as a pony wall, in a shower is practical for many reasons. Here, it affords some privacy, showcases the rain showerhead, lets in light from the rest of the room, and creates a space for towel storage. It also prevents the shower from feeling closed off and tunnellike.

THE
OFFICE

Whether it's mission control for your business, an occasional satellite office to keep you up-to-date, or a family zone to keep your household running like a well-oiled machine, carving out space for a dedicated work area is a great way to keep you organized. Whether big or small, individual or shared, a home office allows you to make the rules for how and when you work and encourages you to express your style and make the office environment a well-appointed work zone that inspires efficiency to help you get the job done.

SERENE SANCTUARY

If you aren't working in a cubicle and don't need to conform to standard office-furniture designs, you can embrace a design aesthetic that suits you. Whether your taste runs to contemporary or classical, try to outfit your office space with elements that are appealing to you and inspire you to get the job done. Even a small home-office space that needs to double as a shared his-and-hers den can be well organized for the workday and then transition into a comfortable after-work aerie if all the elements are in the right place.

DEFINE YOUR CORPORATE STYLE ←•

Draw a line in the sand between comfortable and corporate. Before racing out to buy an oversized "executive" desk without any personality or soul, why not think about how you work, when you work, and what you really need. In the digital age, most of us have far less paper, work on a laptop, and need less desk space than those who handle masses of paper and documents daily. Start by making a list of all the things you want your office to have, and see if it's possible to balance priorities and scale to fit it all in.

PRESENT A UNIFIED FRONT ←•

Match your metal tones and create unity amongst a collection of distinctly different furniture pieces by replating the handles and hardware. If you're trying to mix new with vintage and struggling with different metal finishes, you can remove the old knobs and have them replated for about $10 per piece in your choice of finish. It's a terrific way to update an inexpensive desk find and make it look au courant.

TWO IS BETTER THAN ONE ⬍

There's no rule that dictates the use of only one fabric on a piece of upholstered furniture. When torn between two great fabrics, I try to use both! Covering the frames of the chaises in plush chenille makes them soft and inviting, while choosing prewashed linen for the seat cushions makes them practical and easy to care for. Piping the frames of the chaises in the seat fabric ties the scheme together and accentuates the streamlined silhouette.

CHILL OUT CHAISES ⬍

By being practical and honest about how you'll use the room, you may realize that your little office is not where you'll be entertaining friends and family, so there's no need for seating to accommodate four to six people. If two is all you expect, a pair of luxurious chaise longues that invite you to veg out at the end of a long day (or just recline during a long phone call) are an unexpected and creative furniture solution.

PLAN TO RELAX ⭥

If you don't need to dedicate the entire room to office furniture, you can
carve out that ideal work/life balance by incorporating a den/lounge focus
into the mix. By ensuring that all the support pieces offer extra storage
(such as side tables with drawers, a media console with doors and a shelf,
or a desk with ample drawer storage), you'll be able to store lots of books
and documents, yet your workspace will still look organized and efficient.

—

AMP UP THE ACCENTS ⭥

The addition of decorative fabrics and elegant wallpaper helps add another
element of differentiation between the banal cubicle "environment" and the
personalized workplace that will inspire your best work every day!

MANAGE A PROBLEM AREA ⬍
Cove ceilings make paint choices tricky, as they blur the line
between walls and ceilings. Adding a trim profile around the perimeter
of the room allows you to delineate which areas you want to treat as walls
and which ones become ceiling. Installing the trim band about five feet above
the floor creates the opportunity to install decorative wallpaper below
and a pretty paint colour above.

MAKE THE MOST OF WHAT YOU'VE GOT ➘
If your office has a closet, you can easily turn it into valuable space
for customized storage solutions. By removing the standard clothes-hanging rod
and replacing it with wooden shelves and dividers (painted in a snazzy colour
scheme to complement the room), you can carve out a niche to store files,
supplies, technology, and all sorts of office necessities that would otherwise
create visual clutter. When you are ready to leave the office and turn the
room into a cozy den, simply shut the door and it disappears.

CONQUER THE CLUTTER ↕

If you like to spread out and work across multiple surfaces at once,
consider the added benefit of a console table. The extra tabletop area
offered by a console that floats behind your main desk surface will allow
you to keep your desk on the small side while still giving flexibility
for oodles of paper! Choosing a console with a shelf across
the bottom and pencil drawers at the top will help you keep all of your
supplies easily stashed out of sight when the workday wraps up.

OCEAN VIEW OFFICE

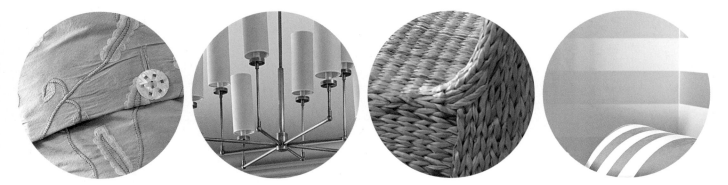

Shared spaces become appealing to both men and women when they incorporate a thoughtful balance of both masculine and feminine elements. This home office has a cool, masculine palette reinforced by wide awning-stripe fabric and chocolate tones, yet maintains a feminine softness with luxurious silk fabrics, pale blue accents, and a delicately patterned area rug. With well-appointed amenities, both Mr. and Mrs. are equally at home in this office!

CHANGE DIRECTION ←
Wallpaper is generally intended to run vertically from floor to ceiling, but no hard rule says you can't run it in any direction. You may want to see what happens when you turn a wallpaper on its side. Some of my favourite wide-striped wallpapers actually look better when installed horizontally instead of vertically. If you are trying to achieve a more contemporary look, a wide stripe is an effective way to add graphic interest to your walls.

ACCENT BOOKSHELVES ←
For a departure from monochromatic bookcases, I painted the beadboard panelling on the back of the bookshelves in delicate robin's-egg blue as a reference to the fabric scheme, and also

as a playful nod to the framed antique engravings of eggs. Instead of an entire wall composed of shelves, you might want to keep the centre section open to allow a place to hang a treasured piece of art. It takes far more books than you might think to fill your shelves completely, and the variation might be a welcome breather.

DON'T SHOW IT ALL OFF ↘
Instead of installing bookshelves that are open from floor to ceiling, consider a breakfront configuration with doors on the lower section. This division between open and closed storage allows you to make the lower section deeper to accommodate boxes and bulky items and also creates a useful ledge at table height.

IMPROVE YOUR OUTLOOK ↕

When designing office spaces, I always try to put the desk in a place where you can enjoy the view and be inspired. Looking out at a garden is far more interesting than staring at a wall, and placing your computer screen in front of the window will eliminate glare on your screen.

DESIGN IS IN THE DETAILS ↕

The little things in a room can make a huge difference in your daily enjoyment of your home. Every element you choose for your interiors has a cumulative effect on the overall product, so don't overlook any of the finishing touches as too small to matter. Sometimes the small details are the ones you touch daily,

so the tactile experience should be pleasing. Hardware, fabrics, carpets, and desk accessories should be a delight to behold and to hold.

CONNECT WITH THE ELEMENTS ↕

When working on spaces by water, such as this one with long views out to the ocean, the goal is to reference and embrace the coastal influences without letting them become a hokey theme. The soft blues allude to a watery palette, the rough woven fibres and textural fabrics give the room an earthy grounding, and the luxurious details create a dynamic mix of textures and textiles that are soothing and sophisticated.

SUNNY HOME OFFICE

With wireless Internet, your home office can be wherever you choose to sit. That's fine if you live in a paper-less world and can concentrate amidst the chaos of daily life, but it's a bit easier to keep track of household finances and meet important deadlines if you have a dedicated workspace. Combining your home office with a den or lounge allows you to create a dual-purpose space whether you are on or off the clock, but making a multifunctional room both relaxing to hang out in and conducive to business activities requires clever solutions to keep your work/life balance in check. A sunny palette and flexible furniture solutions turned this run-down room into a fashionable home headquarters.

ROOM WITH A VIEW ⇒

To make your work area inspiring, place the desk in front of a window. The view will keep you alert, and you won't have to get up out of your chair to daydream. I've always thought that gazing at the sky was more conducive to innovative thinking than staring at a blank wall. If your home office is part den like this one, make sure to create a look that works together in harmony and orient the room so you aren't staring at your "office" while trying to relax and unwind or watch TV.

TABLE TALK ⇒

It's nice to think you could just set up your laptop on a table and call it an office, but the reality is that a desk needs drawers to work for most of us. Without a number of drawers to tuck away papers and necessities, your desk surface will likely become overrun with papers, which will likely become distracting (and, if you are anything like me, may lead to procrastination while you tidy up). You'll have to find the model that's right for you, but a smaller desk with lots of drawer space may prove to be a better investment than a big one with less storage.

GO WIRELESS ↕

For a small investment, you can rid yourself of the tangle and trip hazard of cords. Your printer, fax, and any other wireless devices can be hidden behind closed doors, thereby freeing up precious desk space. A vintage cabinet, sideboard, or armoire can be divided up to accommodate all your technology and office supplies. Pull-out drawers can easily be divided into compartments using strips of wood to keep all your paper, envelopes, and stationery organized. Think about what you actually need before you install it.

KEEP IT LIGHT ⇒

Let the boardrooms and executive offices use the classic banker's palette of dark mahogany, forest green, and oxblood leather. Opt for a scheme that is sunny, cheery, and bright so your office is a place that wakes you up. The bubbly energy of the yellow and cream graffiti print sets the tone for the room—but remember, a little bold colour goes a long way, so limit your use to impactful accents instead of overall application. I like colour best when tempered with plenty of white and cream, even on wood furniture, and like to use glossy white paint to unify dark mahogany and dated golden oak.

CERULEAN CRAFT ROOM

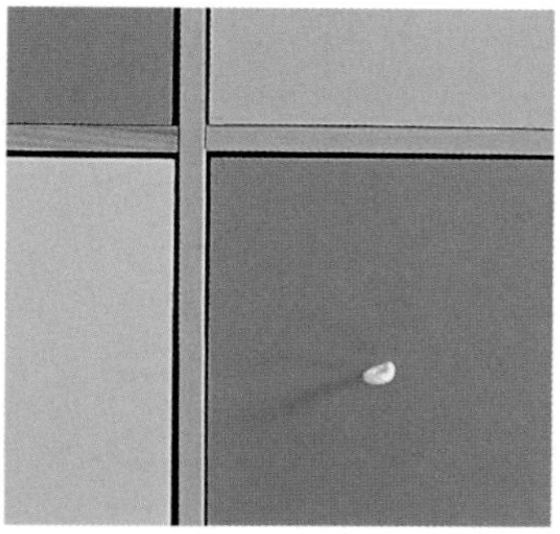

Whether or not you fancy yourself a DIY enthusiast or an avid crafter, crafting has become a popular pastime and an active pursuit for a large part of the population. Having a hobby that stimulates creativity and reduces time spent in front of a screen is a worthwhile endeavour, so I embraced all creative pursuits when designing a multipurpose workspace for the entire family that offers a place to do work, homework, school projects, gift wrapping, and to have fun with arts and crafts.

MAXIMIZE YOUR OPTIONS ➻

Instead of customizing your craft area with inflexible built-in solutions, focus on maintaining maximum flexibility for the future. Freestanding desks (which are actually kitchen islands complete with butcher-block tops) can be rearranged depending on the project and offer plenty of seating for up to four people at a time. With open shelves, baskets filled with supplies can be kept close at hand to facilitate easy access (and even easier cleanup).

BE A SMART COOKIE ➻

One of the most durable work surfaces is a butcher-block counter. It's also an economical choice that is easy to maintain, so it makes sense to reallocate this tried-and-true kitchen material to your work area. If you leave the wood untreated, it can be sanded down to remove marks and scratches, or you can treat the butcher block with water-based urethane before setting up shop, and the counters will be easy to wipe down and keep clean whenever your creativity results in a messy countertop.

PLAY WITH PATTERN ➻

A custom tackboard that covers one large wall is the optimal place to bring a touch of texture and bold pattern to a room that is otherwise streamlined and efficiency oriented. With a sleek steel frame, this board complements the cool metal accents that tie the room together, and the large surface allows space to showcase everyone's creations.

SORT AND STORE ↕

My rule is "if in doubt, label it." When a number of people are sharing a single space, organization helps limit chaos. Overscaled chrome drawer labels can easily be affixed to the face of any unit with drawers (and come in a variety of styles and finishes to suit your decor), so you'll never be left scrambling to find the supplies you need. Jazz up plain slab-front drawers with oversized square knobs, and your style statement will be snazzy instead of staid.

—

CLEAR THE DECK ↕

One thing I've learned about creative projects is that they tend to spread — they inevitably take over all available space . . . and then some. So, try to keep your supplies and tools within easy reach, yet off your work surface. Wall systems that are generally geared to kitchen storage are ideally suited to the diverse array of materials you'll need to store. Having a variety of containers sized to suit also comes in handy.

PEEKABOO ⬍

Reimagine a magnetic, wall-hung spice rack as a see-through
installation for little bits and bobs. Tiny trinkets, buttons, and beads
are easier to manage when they can be sorted into small, glass-topped
containers and look both colourful and cool on the wall.

ADD A LITTLE DIY ⬍

Start your creative incubator off with a crafty storage solution.
Incorporate your chosen colour theme into your room by painting the
fronts of a simple set of storage drawers with a variety of hues. With minimal
investment of time, a collection of little drawers becomes a colourful charmer.

KIDS' ATTIC ESCAPE

One of my favourite characteristics of old houses is that they often have quirky little rooms just waiting to be interpreted as more than just leftover space. As a kid, I dreamed of having a house with a turret (what little princess didn't?). Enclosed porches, sunrooms, dormers, and turrets not only add to the curb appeal of a home but also offer unusual interior spaces that inspire innovative self-expression in design. Take this teensy room as an example. Too small to be a useful bedroom, it would make an ideal kids' homework/lounge area, I figured.

BUILD IT, DON'T BUY IT ⭥
If space is at a premium, I prefer everything built-in, like the interior of a ship. If you designate space for all you wish to store, it will be easier to keep it tidy.

STICK WITH THE CLASSICS ⭥
When looking for an inexpensive way to build out, you'll find it's easier to achieve winning results if you stick to a more traditional style. Contemporary details require perfection and look sloppy if not executed perfectly, but a variety of decorative trim profiles can lead your DIY project to dramatic results if you keep it classic.

BUY THE BEST ⭥
Start any DIY project by investing in the best materials available at your building supply store. If installing shelves, be sure to use cabinet-grade plywood and install a facing that is at least an inch thick across the front to keep your shelves from sagging under the weight of your books.

THINK DOUBLE DUTY ⭥
Building a little reading nook/daybed in front of the bookshelf provides a great spot to curl up with a book or a laptop and even doubles as an extra bed when guests are visiting. Choose a single seat cushion made from foam that's at least 4 inches thick, and your guests will actually find it comfortable. Make

sure all the fabrics you select are durable and washable. Choose 100 percent cotton and prewash and preshrink your fabrics before you get them sewn up. This way you'll be able to toss them in the washer and dryer when they get dirty.

BE QUIET ⭢
I'm a fan of hardwood floors, but often avoid them in small spaces. If you want the room to be cozy and quiet, wall-to-wall broadloom with a short, dense pile is a good plan. If you go for wood, you'll inevitably want to add a rug for warmth in the chilly months, which may just catch the legs of your chair every time you pull into or push back from the desk.

GET INSPIRED ⭢
I believe the best location for the desk relates to the view. Writer's block is far less likely to set in and mundane tasks are made more enjoyable if daydreaming and inspiration are encouraged by placing the desk in front of a window. Building a desk into a bay window is remarkably easy. Template the profile of the bay with cardboard, then cut the desktop out of cabinet-grade, $3/4$-inch-thick plywood. Trim the front with shingle moulding, add some decorative iron brackets to reinforce the sides, and drill a hole in the top to keep cords organized. Voilà — the closet-sized room becomes the ideal office nook.

ACKNOWLEDGEMENTS

I have a lot of people to thank, and a lot to be thankful for. Here goes . . .

This book has been over a decade in the making and is the result of countless thousands of hours of time and energy invested by talented and dedicated craftspeople and skilled trades to realize the transformation of each and every room within these pages. Yes, it's safe to say that this book is the product of blood, sweat, and tears (if you've ever watched my TV shows, you know exactly what I'm talking about . . .). Our craft is a product of human time and effort, and without the work of all the **trades**, **craftspeople**, **manufacturers**, and **suppliers** who contributed their expertise to transform ordinary spaces into extraordinary places, none of this would be possible. For all you have done to help me make our ideas become reality, thanks to each and every one of you. I hope you look at these pages with pride, knowing that you made a difference.

But before the magic can happen, it all begins with the **clients**, without whom none of this would exist. A huge thanks to every client who invited us in, embraced the creative vision, invested in our ideas (even when you wondered what on earth we were thinking), and allowed us to transform your home into a new vision of you and your personal style. Your involvement in the project is what gives each room a unique and individual flavour, and your willingness to invite us in to your personal space has fuelled our creative process.

In the early days of your career, you never know who you'll meet when you go to work, and what their impact will be. On one of my early photo shoots, I met **Stacey Brandford**, and soon learned that not only was he an unflappable, cool and competent photographer, with an unwavering ability to deliver an endless supply of beautiful shots, but collaborative and just plain fun to be around. Creating an entire book with the work we shot together is a testament to how extraordinary I think Stacey is. Behind every great photographer is a talented team, and **Mikael Cosmo** and **Ryan Coe** are the men behind the Stacey machine, who make every shot sparkle.

After ensuring every room looks picture perfect, there's the matter of making the girl in the room look half as good as her surroundings. **Brandon Barré** has a unique knack for knowing just how to light and just when to click the shutter so that this aging mom of two looks a little bit more youthful and a lot more well rested than I often feel in reality on a shoot day. Thanks for sharing the portraits for this book.

You are only as good as your weakest link, and I have the best team. My collaborators and colleagues at Sarah Richardson Design made each of these rooms a reality, and this book is a shared accomplishment. Whether calling couriers or finding the perfect finishing touch, it takes a co-ordinated team effort to drive any space across the finish line, and I'm thankful for everyone who has been a part of the SRD team and helped take our projects to the next level. Specifically, to **Natalie Hodgins**, **Lindsay Mens**, **Tommy Smythe**, **Kate Stuart**, **Allison Willson**, **Tara Finlay**, **Nicole Herman**, and **Tanya Bonus**—you are talented designers blessed with endless style and fabulous ideas, and our clients live their lives in incredible spaces every day thanks to your passion and hard work. These pages are our pages, and they tell the stories of our many adventures and experiments as a team.

Good partnerships lead to great results. My partnership through five TV series and over fifteen years with **Michael Prini** and Primevista Television allowed me to chart my design destiny with someone who was just as dedicated to the production details as I was to to the rooms and visuals. There isn't a more invested or attentive producer out there, and your unwavering dedication to making great TV is a huge part of the reason this book exists.

You can't have a show without a network, and **HGTV** has given me the platform to share my ideas with anyone willing to watch or listen to them. To everyone in the big HGTV family that I've worked with over all these years (including Barb Williams, Emily Morgan, Tanya Linton, Andrea Griffith, Robert Wimbish, Bill Myers, Karen Gelbart, Michelle Kosoy, Anna Gecan, and Jenna Keane), thanks for helping us deliver real-life design solutions to viewers around the world that could stand the test of time and become the foundation for this book.

A television crew is expected to guide the technical process, but my production crew has always been a cut above the rest, and lugged, dusted, vacuumed, assembled, and installed whatever was needed to make the rooms we worked on picture perfect. Going beyond the call of duty is just who you are, but your appreciation of the transformation from beginning to end always made me feel proud. **Rick Boston**, **Michael Josselyn**, and **Mikey Mazeika**—you're my favourite cheerleaders!

This book was a decade in the making because getting it out of my head and onto the pages in a way that I imagined it didn't seem possible until I met the delightful, calm, capable, and creative talents of **Rose Pereira**, who managed to know exactly what I was dreaming of, and then exceeded my expectations to design the book you hold in your hands. I'm sorry for the relentless late nights and excessive amounts of caffeine you had to ingest to bring this project to life, but I am deeply grateful and very proud of where we've ended up. Additional thanks to **Erica Rodrigues** for her design assistance.

Once I knew what it looked like, finding the right home for my book was a voyage of discovery, but as soon as I met **Kevin Hanson** at Simon & Schuster Canada, I knew the search was over. Thanks to **Alison Clarke**, **David Millar**, **Felicia Quon**, **Amy Cormier**, **Rita Silva**, and the S&S Canada team for not only jumping at the chance to make this book, but making the process a fun adventure. Your passion for the written word is inspiring, and I'm honoured to have made the cut amongst all the real authors you've worked with.

Since design is a worldwide market, I was intent on taking my ideas to a global audience, and thanks to some help from the S&S Canada team, we somehow convinced **Louise Burke**, **Jennifer Bergstrom**, **Jean Anne Rose**, and the Gallery Books division of Simon & Schuster in New York into taking a chance on a girl from Canada. Here's hoping that gamble pays off in the free trade spectrum.

I am a designer, creative spirit, and a DIYer in the overall game of life, so it was important to me that the words on these pages be written by me (looking back, during the writing process I must admit to wondering . . . all these words . . . what on earth was I thinking?). I thought editors were supposed to be serious and tough, but fortunately they broke the mould when they made **Tricia Boczkowski**, and I got a fun, easygoing, and super supportive editor to champion my amateur writing abilities. Phew!

Every girl needs a gay BFF, but I've got more that. **Tommy Smythe**, without your collaboration, design vision, and impeccable taste, I never would have made it through over 300 renovations on TV, we definitely wouldn't have laughed so hard (and I would not have blushed nearly so often). Your wit and wisdom, friendship, and loyalty go far beyond the definition of any colleague and have made you my co-host, sounding board, style counsel, day husband and creative collaborator. This book would not have been possible without you, and I value all the insights and energy you've invested at every step of the way from inception to completion. Thanks for always being there and never settling for less than the best.

And every good on-camera team needs an engine behind the scenes that makes the process run smoothly, even when the train seems to be heading down the wrong track. If you've ever wondered how we make it look so easy on TV, I can tell you that **Lindsay Mens** likely has something to do with it. With lightning speed and endless charm and cheeriness, this girl can and has moved mountains for me to get the job done.

Spending your career making homes fabulous for other people isn't without its perils. It's not all sunshine and happy days, and sometimes it seems that nothing will go right, and the job will never be done (or done right). Thanks to my amazing husband, **Alexander Younger**, for steering me through the ups and downs of fifteen years and seventeen seasons of TV production, and helping me keep the big picture in perspective with your sound advice and support, and of course for never complaining when you came home to find the house torn apart, repainted, or reconfigured . . . yet again.

There's no handbook to being an entrepreneur and a TV personality in an ever-changing market, so thanks to my girls, my confidantes and my besties **Natalie Hodgins**, **Stephanie Nerlich**, and **Eva Salem** for being there for over two decades as we all try to figure out the secrets to success day by day.

Spreading the good word about a brand or an individual is no easy task in a noisy world, but **Deb McCain**, pint-sized PR powerhouse extraordinaire, somehow makes all my design adventures newsworthy and noteworthy. Thanks for helping strategically steer my ship towards interesting opportunities by being the most savvy "in the know" girl I know.

I am a firm believer that a house needs to have a soul, and that embracing original art infuses character and spirit into a home. Thanks to the talented **artists**, and the **galleries** that represent them, who help to fill our clients' homes with unique and beautiful works of art, including Michael Adamson, Canvas Gallery (Chris Albert, Donna Andreychuk, Sophia Banks, Meredith Bingham, Mark Brodkin, Wendy Farrow, Roz Hermant, Ben Mark Holzberg, Steven Nederveen, George Pavlasek, Charlene Serdan, Marjolyn Van der Hart), Ingram Gallery (Barker Fairley, Patricia Larsen), Loch Gallery (Bogdan Molea), Nicholas Metivier Gallery (John Hartman, Douglas Walker), Christine Flynn, Dave Hind, Tony Koukos, and Wieslaw Michalak.

The goal of the work we create is to design interiors that will speak to a global audience. Some of the rooms within the pages have previously appeared in other publications, so thanks to *Canadian House and Home* and *Renovation Style* for allowing these images to have a second life and be part of my design story in this book.

And there's no point writing a book if no one is going to read it or buy it, so mostly, thanks to **you** for watching, reading, and engaging with my work for almost two decades. You are the reason I keep going, and you keep me focused on the authentic spirit of home. Cheers to you!